MAR    2010

# HISTORY OF
# THE ANCIENT AND MEDIEVAL WORLD

## SECOND EDITION

## VOLUME 3

## ANCIENT GREECE

**Marshall Cavendish**
Reference
New York

Marshall Cavendish
99 White Plains Road
Tarrytown, New York 10591

www.marshallcavendish.us

**Library of Congress Cataloging-in-Publication Data**

History of the ancient and medieval world / [edited by Henk Dijkstra]. --
2nd ed.
     v. cm.
  Includes bibliographical references and index.
  Contents: v. 1. The first civilizations -- v. 2. Western Asia and the
Mediterranean -- v. 3. Ancient Greece -- v. 4. The Roman Empire -- v. 5. The
changing shape of Europe -- v. 6. The early Middle Ages in western Asia and
Europe -- v. 7. Southern and eastern Asia -- v. 8. Europe in the Middle Ages
-- v. 9. Western Asia, northern Europe, and Africa in the Middle Ages -- v.
10. The passing of the medieval world -- v. 11. Index.
  ISBN 978-0-7614-7789-1 (set) -- ISBN 978-0-7614-7791-4 (v. 1) -- ISBN
978-0-7614-7792-1 (v. 2) -- ISBN 978-0-7614-7793-8 (v. 3) -- ISBN
978-0-7614-7794-5 (v. 4) -- ISBN 978-0-7614-7795-2 (v. 5) -- ISBN
978-0-7614-7796-9 (v. 6) -- ISBN 978-0-7614-7797-6 (v. 7) -- ISBN
978-0-7614-7798-3 (v. 8) -- ISBN 978-0-7614-7799-0 (v. 9) -- ISBN
978-0-7614-7800-3 (v. 10) -- ISBN 978-0-7614-7801-0 (v. 11)
  1. History, Ancient. 2. Middle Ages. 3. Civilization, Medieval. I.
Dijkstra, Henk.
  D117.H57 2009
  940.1--dc22

                              2008060052


Printed in Malaysia

12 11 10 09 08  7 6 5 4 3 2 1

General Editor: Henk Dijkstra

**Marshall Cavendish**
Project Editor: Brian Kinsey
Publisher: Paul Bernabeo
Production Manager: Michael Esposito

**Brown Reference Group**
Project Editor: Chris King
Text Editors: Shona Grimbly, Charles Phillips
Designer: Lynne Lennon
Cartographers: Joan Curtis, Darren Awuah
Picture Researcher: Laila Torsun
Indexer: Christine Michaud
Managing Editor: Tim Cooke

## PICTURE CREDITS

# SET CONTENTS

# VOLUME CONTENTS

# FROM TYRANNY TO DEMOCRACY

In the seventh and sixth centuries BCE, Greece saw the rise of tyranny as a system of government when politicians such as Cypselus in Corinth and Peisistratus in Athens gained power. Later, a new form of democracy arose in Athens.

During the Archaic period (c. 750–500 BCE), there was much social unrest in the burgeoning city-states of Greece. Some of this unrest was relieved by colonization, while attempts were made at home to reduce the gap between rich and poor. For example, in Athens in the sixth century BCE, the lawgiver Solon specifically addressed the rights of the poor by abolishing debt slavery. Another way of dealing with the internal social problems in the Greek communities was the institution of tyranny.

The word *tyrannos* was not originally Greek; it was borrowed from the Lydian language and was used to refer to an absolute ruler who had taken power illegally. Such a ruler was not necessarily a "tyrant" in the modern sense of the word, since an unlawful sovereign was not necessarily a cruel or unjust one. However, the fact that the Greeks adopted a foreign word for this new political phenomenon indicated that they viewed it as alien to the idea of a *polis* (city-state) as a community of citizens.

## The age of the tyrants

During the Archaic period, individual aristocrats all over Greece took advantage of infighting among the nobility to seize power. In most cases, the details of how they came to power are not known, but what evidence there is suggests there may have been military coups. The new tyrants had clearly received support from aristocratic friends and followers, and sometimes from another state. They may also have used mercenary troops, which were a new phenomenon at the time. To win the support of the populace, they often promised various rewards, such as grants of land, thereby turning social discontent to their own advantage.

One of the first tyrants was Cypselus. Around 657 BCE, he drove out the ruling aristocracy in Corinth. During the next 150 years, tyranny became the most common form of government in the Greek world; of the more important city-states only Sparta and Aegina appear to have escaped it. Many of these tyrants were quite popular, particularly among the middle-class, mercantile populace who had been denied any social privileges by the previous aristocratic rule. Some tyrants were also popular because they stimulated local patriotism and organized cults and festivals that celebrated the local gods.

The tyrannies followed a similar pattern in each state. Eventually, popular feeling would move against a dictatorship, as councils and tribal meetings were excluded from power and the tyrant placed himself above the law.

Most tyrants decreed their rule hereditary, but the people tended to

*This bust depicts the tyrant Periander, who ruled the city of Corinth between 625 and 585 BCE.*

unite against the second or third generation. As resistance against a tyrant increased, he would typically take harsh measures in an attempt to remain in power. However, the will of the people would eventually prevail, and he would be ousted. One result of the phenomenon of tyranny was that by undermining the position of the aristocracy, it paved the way for democracy.

## The tyranny in Corinth

After around 750 BCE, Corinth became the most important port and the most prosperous city in Greece. Its situation on the south of the isthmus joining central Greece to the Peloponnese made Corinth a crucial trading point. It had harbors on both sides of the isthmus, and to avoid the dangerous journey around the Peloponnese, many traders arranged

# THE GREEK WORLD IN THE SIXTH CENTURY BCE

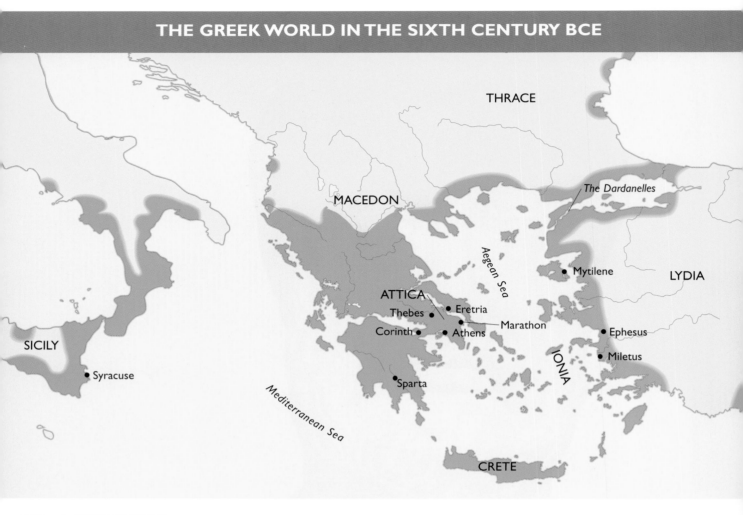

THRACE

MACEDON

*The Dardanelles*

*Aegean Sea*

Mytilene

LYDIA

ATTICA

Thebes •  • Eretria

Corinth •  • Athens — Marathon

Ephesus

SICILY

Miletus

IONIA

• Syracuse

• Sparta

*Mediterranean Sea*

CRETE

## KEY

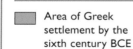

Area of Greek settlement by the sixth century BCE

for their goods to be transferred at Corinth to wagons to be transported to the other side, where they could be shipped again. Trade with states on the eastern shores of the Mediterranean Sea thrived, and after the Greek colonization of southern Italy and Sicily, trade with the west increased as well.

Corinth was also the center of a prosperous export industry in earthenware. Corinthian pottery, painted in exquisite detail, was shipped out to destinations in every direction, outselling any other pottery of the time. Most of this commercial activity was dominated by the Bacchiad family, an aristocratic clan that ruled over Corinth.

Around 657 BCE, the resentment of the mercantile class against the Bacchiads

boiled over into revolution, and a new leader called Cypselus was put in place as a tyrant. Cypselus proved himself to be a mild and popular dictator, who needed no bodyguard. According to a popular legend about his birth, Cypselus was a hero favored by the gods. He belonged to the same class as the aristocracy and yet was an outsider.

## The rule of Periander

Under Cypselus and, later, his son Periander, the prosperity of Corinth reached new highs. Colonies were founded on the eastern coast of the Adriatic Sea, to develop the trade route to Italy. Periander built a slipway 5 miles (8 km) long across the isthmus so ships could be put on trolleys and dragged

## THE LEGEND OF CYPSELUS'S BIRTH

One legend that became popular in Corinth after Cypselus came to power tells the story of his birth.

Cypselus's mother, Labda, was a member of the Bacchiad clan but had been rejected by her family because of a handicap. She married a stranger named Eetion and bore him a son. Oracles prophesied that the child would grow up to destroy the ruling dynasty. When members of the Bacchiad clan heard of this, they arrived at the child's home with the intention of killing him.

However, his mother hid the infant in a wooden chest, called a *kypsele* in Greek, and the child escaped. Taking his name from the word *kypsele*, Cypselus grew up in a village outside Corinth. When he became an adult, another oracle ordered him to return to the city and seize power from the ruling Bacchiads.

This legend is similar to many others in which an infant is hunted but survives, later to become a great ruler. The story of Moses in the Bible is just one such tale.

*This ancient road leads from the ruins of the Greek city of Corinth.*

*This Corinthian tile depicts a potter standing in front of a kiln. Corinth was famous for its pottery in the seventh century BCE.*

from one side to the other. The tolls from this facility greatly increased the city's wealth.

Periander ruled from 625 to 585 BCE and showed himself to be a wily statesman. He extended the power of Corinth both by the sword and by diplomacy. When Mytilene and Athens were in dispute over the ownership of a colony in 600 BCE, Periander was asked to adjudicate between them. He came down on the side of Athens, which made the city a valuable ally.

During Periander's reign, Corinth also became a center of culture, where poets and musicians congregated. He inaugurated many public building works, giving rise to the architectural style known as the Doric order.

However, the rule of Periander had a darker side. He was subject to violent mood swings, and he was ruthless in executing anyone he thought threatened his

power. His actions, as related by the fifth-century-BCE historian Herodotus, caused his tyranny to deteriorate into a reign of terror.

Periander died in 585 BCE and was succeeded by his nephew Psammetichus, who was deposed following a rebellion in the third year of his reign. The government of Corinth was then taken over by a group of aristocrats, who established an oligarchy (rule by an elite).

## The tyranny in Athens

Although the inspired lawgiver Solon had produced a new code of law for Athens in the early sixth century BCE, it was still far from becoming a democracy. Solon had granted civil rights to the poorer Athenians and put an end to debt slavery, but he had done little to secure the economic future of the poor. Rivalry between landed and landless people continued, as did rivalry within the aristoc-

## THE DOWNFALL OF PERIANDER

This anecdote from the historian Herodotus describes the downfall of the tyranny in Corinth:

"Periander sent an envoy to the tyrant Thrasybulus of Miletus to ask him the best way to rule without conflict. Thrasybulus took a walk through a cornfield with the envoy, while questioning him about the situation in Corinth. Now and then the tyrant would stop and cut off the largest ears of corn that rose above the others. In this way he destroyed the best of the corn, and he later sent the envoy away without having given him an answer.

"When the envoy returned to Corinth, Periander asked him what Thrasybulus had advised. The envoy replied that he had received no answer, and he also expressed surprise that Periander had sent him to a man who had nothing better to do than destroy the best part of his crop. But Periander understood immediately what Thrasybulus had meant by this action. Believing that this represented the punishment of the most important citizens of Corinth, from that moment he started treating the aristocrats and the rich with extreme cruelty."

*The Temple of Apollo is one of the most famous ruins in the ancient Greek city of Corinth. Corinth was one of the most prosperous Greek cities in the seventh century BCE.*

**The Acropolis in Athens was a focal point of the city during the reign of the tyrant Peisistratus.**

racy. Against this unsettled background, a politician called Peisistratus gained the support of the common people and managed to seize power in a coup described by Herodotus:

"At that time [561 BCE] a civil war was raging in Attica between the coastal party and the plains party. Taking advantage of their quarrel, Peisistratus devised a plan to become tyrant of Athens by forming a third party. This was the party from over the hills. He mobilized a group of followers and won victory by means of a clever trick. One day he wounded himself before coming to the market. There, he said that he had miraculously escaped from his enemies, who had tried to kill him. To protect himself from further attacks, he asked for an official bodyguard. The Athenians gave him permission to arm a group of 300 citizens with clubs. With the aid of these people Peisistratus rebelled and succeeded in capturing first the Acropolis and subsequently the seat of government."

The plains party referred to by Herodotus consisted of old, aristocratic families from the region surrounding the city of Athens. The coastal party was more democratic and consisted of several families, the most important of which were the Alcmaeonidae. Their domain lay along the coast to the south of Athens. Peisistratus's party "from over the hills" was probably a splinter group from the coastal party. The phrase "over the hills" may refer to Peisistratus's power base on the east coast of Attica, on the other side (from Athens) of the Hymettos Mountain ridge.

## The return of Peisistratus

Soon after Peisistratus had established himself as the tyrant of Athens, however, he was driven out again by the two rival groups of aristocrats. Five years later, he returned from exile and to power with the help of his former rival Megacles. Herodotus described what happened as follows:

"As soon as Peisistratus had left, the two groups who had banished him began to quarrel. Finally Megacles, the leader of the coastal party, sent an envoy to Peisistratus. Peisistratus would be returned to power if he agreed to marry the daughter of Megacles. Peisistratus agreed to the proposal, and together they designed a plan to accomplish the return of the tyrant."

This plan involved dressing up a woman as the goddess Pallas Athena, guardian of the city of Athens, and arranging for her to travel through the city, preceded by heralds who announced that the goddess was leading Peisistratus back to his rightful place. The plan appears to have worked. For a while, Peisistratus resumed his role as tyrant, but the alliance with the coastal party and the marriage to Megacles's daughter soon broke down. Once again, Peisistratus was forced to flee Athens.

During the following decade, Peisistratus first accumulated a great deal of wealth, mainly from the gold and silver mines in Thrace. He then concentrated on building good relations with states and individuals who might be prepared to supply funds and mercenaries to support his planned coup in Athens. In 546 BCE, he landed with an army at Marathon, on the east coast of Attica. Marching towards Athens, he was joined by other disaffected forces. The Athenians sent out an army to meet him, and at the Battle of Pallene, Peisistratus was victorious. He entered Athens as its tyrant and this time remained in power for more than 19 years.

## The rule of Peisistratus

Peisistratus was a benign tyrant. He took no revenge against his opponents, and he upheld the laws laid down by Solon. He imposed very moderate taxation on the populace, and, under his rule, trade and industry flourished. In his efforts to make Athens the political center of Attica, Peisistratus organized great "national" religious festivals, such as the Dionysian festivals at which tragedies were performed. The Panathenaea—the celebration of the city goddess Pallas Athena—was also turned into a great festival. The *Iliad* and the *Odyssey*, the two great epic poems of Homer, were recited at this and other events.

An important social institution introduced by Peisistratus was the one of traveling judges, who visited the villages of Attica, listened to cases, and dispensed justice. Peisistratus also initiated a great road-building program, which made communicating and traveling around Attica much easier in general.

Many substantial construction projects were also undertaken to emphasize the great importance of Athens and its ruling family. Poorer Athenians seem to have benefited under his rule from a redistribution of land, as well as from the stimulation of trade and industry. The pottery industry in particular flourished. During Peisistratus's rule, Athenian black-figure pottery came to supersede all other pottery on the Mediterranean markets.

## Hippias

Peisistratus was succeeded in 527 BCE by his son Hippias (see box, page 305), who continued his father's policy of making

*This bronze statue depicting the god Zeus dates to the early fifth century BCE. Zeus was king of the Greek gods.*

301

*This vase illustration shows a farmer plowing a field. Farming methods were relatively primitive in ancient Greece.*

Athens a cultural center. However, opposition to his rule was growing. The powerful family of the Alcmaeonidae had gathered together a large group of exiles on the Peloponnese. These disaffected Athenians managed to gain the support of the Spartans, who were trying to expand their territory northward. A Spartan army joined in an invasion of Attica in 510 BCE. Hippias and his supporters were trapped on the Acropolis. Hippias was deposed but allowed to go into exile. He subsequently left for a colony in the Dardanelles. His departure brought more than 35 years of Athenian tyranny to an end.

## An agricultural economy

Trade and industry flourished in Greece throughout the time of Cypselus and Peisistratus. However, the main economic activity of most people was agriculture. Some 90 percent of the population were farmers, making a living growing olives, figs, grapes, and fruit, as well as cultivating crops such as grain, beans, and green vegetables.

Farming methods were primitive. Plowing was done by means of a wooden plow drawn by oxen, which, rather than turning the earth, merely scratched the surface. At first, farmers had to leave a field fallow every year or so to allow it to regain fertility, but by around 400 BCE, they had learned the art of crop rotation. Most Greek farms were small, although there was the occasional large holding. The work was carried out by individual farmer-landholders or by tenant farmers or serfs.

Olive oil was a major agricultural product. It was an important source of export revenue, and, at home, it was used universally in cooking and for lamp oil. Olive oil also had a significant part to play in religious ceremonies.

Craftsman had a low status in Archaic Greece. Potters, smiths, tanners, and other craftsmen generally worked in small workshops, which were usually run as a family business. Textile production was a domestic industry carried out by women. Only a small handful of people in each polis could have survived by

## WAR AND COINAGE

The link between war and the economy is illustrated by the fact that the world's first coins were probably produced to pay mercenaries. These coins were minted at the end of the seventh century BCE by the kings of Lydia in Anatolia. The coins were made from pieces of electrum, a natural alloy of gold and silver, and were stamped on one side with a mark that guaranteed their weight, and thus their value.

Around 600 BCE, Greek cities on the coast of Anatolia, notably Ephesus and Miletus, began to mint their own coins. These coins were made of silver and were marked with the stamp of the polis that issued them. Over the next century, this practice of issuing coins was adopted by Greek states in Europe. Under the Athenian tyrants, Athenian coins were issued stamped with the emblem of an owl, representing the goddess Pallas Athena.

While the use of coinage remained limited in Lydia during the sixth century BCE, it acquired great importance in facilitating trade in Greece, and small bronze coins appeared alongside the silver ones. However, the introduction of coinage did not create a full monetary economy. Barter remained the staple form of exchange.

*This illustration from a Greek vase shows a shoemaker at work. Craftsmen such as these were held in low esteem in ancient Greece.*

doing non–agricultural work. The low esteem in which craftsmen were held is summed up by the fourth century-BCE author Xenophon in the following words:

"Craftsmanship has a bad name and is quite rightly greatly despised. . . . It makes such demands on a man that he can no longer devote himself to his friends or to the polis. Such people must be bad friends and bad defenders of their nation. . . . The best occupations are farming and the waging of war."

Working at a trade seems to have been equated with a lack of freedom. The work of the farmer was rated more highly than that of the "wage slave," who was dependent on his employer, or the work of the craftsman or small trader, who was dependent on his customers.

Most trade in Greece at this time was on a very small scale. Such trade as there was was either carried on by farmers, who brought their surplus product to the market, or by craftsmen, who sold their goods to customers in the workshops. Professional traders—those who bought the products of others in order to resell them at a profit—were rare. Only rich merchants engaged in this type of overseas trade, and they were wealthy enough to build their own ships and employ others to undertake the trading voyages. Nevertheless, however small-scale or marginal it was, trade in the Archaic period still offered great opportunities for personal enrichment.

War booty was another important source of income in Archaic Greece. The booty taken on military enterprises provided a major source of wealth for aggressive city-states. With wars waged almost constantly among the many Greek states, booty was probably as important a source of income as agricultural production.

## A return to democracy

After Hippias was deposed in 510 BCE, the aristocrat Cleisthenes (570–508 BCE) seized the opportunity to establish a new democracy based on the political emancipation of the *demos*, or common people. In the words of the fifth-century BCE historian Herodotus: "Cleisthenes made the *demos* his partners."

Cleisthenes was a member of the Alcmaeonid family, the clan that had opposed the tyrant Peisistratus some 50 years earlier. Cleisthenes was the son of

*This Athenian silver coin from the fifth century BCE is stamped with a picture of an owl, the symbol of Pallas Athena, the city's patron goddess.*

Megacles, who had been both an ally and an enemy of the tyrant. The Alcmaeonidae had been exiled several times during the late sixth century BCE; Cleisthenes himself was banished from Athens for some 20 years. He returned to take a prominent part in the overthrow of Hippias.

Cleisthenes instigated a program of political reforms between 510 and 507 BCE. His new constitution, under which the political weight in Athens shifted from the aristocrats to the *demos*, took effect around 502 BCE. A crucial part of his reforms was to improve the civil rights of both the *thetes* (the small landless farmers and day workers) and the *zeugitai* (the economically independent farmers). Under Solon, the *zeugitai* had been allowed political office, and during the reign of tyranny, many of them had become prosperous enough to be able to afford the full suit of armor required to be a hoplite. Their role as hoplites had become increasingly significant; their importance to the military security of the polis was almost certainly an influential factor in Cleisthenes's decision to enlist their political support.

## The Council of 500

The nucleus of Cleisthenes's reforms was the creation of a new institution, the Council of 500, which may have been an extension of an earlier council established by Solon, but with wider powers. The Council of 500 became the pivotal point of political life in Athens, although the ultimate power of decision making lay with the *ecclesia*, or public assembly.

# HIPPIAS, THE LAST ATHENIAN TYRANT

Hippias, the son of Peisistratus, was 40 years old when he succeeded his father in 527 BCE. He ruled with the help of his younger brother, Hipparchus, who was instrumental in bringing two distinguished poets—Anacreon and Simonides—to Athens, strengthening its growing reputation as the cultural center of Greece.

Around 514 BCE, a plot to assassinate both Hippias and Hipparchus was hatched by two young aristocrats, Harmodius and Aristogeiton, who were lovers. The assassination was planned as an act of personal revenge. Hipparchus had apparently made advances to Harmodius but was rejected, spurring Hipparchus to offer a public insult to Harmodius's sister. The assassination plot failed. Only Hipparchus was killed, and in the botched attempt, Harmodius was cut down by Hippias's bodyguard. Aristogeiton was later tortured to death. After this attempt on his life, Hippias ruled with great severity, which accelerated the end of his tyranny. When Hippias was finally deposed, Harmodius and Aristogeiton were hailed as "tyrant killers," and their act was commemorated in an annual religious festival.

After Hippias was forced into exile, he eventually traveled to Persia and obtained an appointment at the royal court as an advisor to Darius I. In 490 BCE, Hippias, approaching 80, returned with the Persian army to Marathon, where he had landed more than 50 years earlier with his father, Peisistratus, and an invading army. The idea was that, after the Persian victory, Hippias would be reinstated as tyrant of Athens, under Persian rule. However, things did not go according to plan—the Athenians defeated the Persians, and Hippias had to flee, along with the remains of the Persian army. Disappointed and disillusioned, the aged tyrant died aboard ship on the return voyage.

*This sculpture depicts the "tyrant killers" Harmodius and Aristogeiton. It is a Roman copy of a statue originally made by the Greek sculptor Kritios.*

*Farmers harvest grapes in this vase illustration from the sixth century BCE.*

coastal, and 10 rural districts. Three districts—one urban, one coastal, and one rural—were then selected and combined into one *phyle*. The resulting *phyle* was a completely artificial unit; its urban, coastal, and rural sections often did not even adjoin. The purpose was to thoroughly mix the population of Attica in order to prevent the rise of regional power. The ten *phylae* formed by Cleisthenes were the basis of all the democratic institutions in Athens.

Soon after Cleisthenes initiated his political reforms, ostracism was introduced. This practice was a means to enable the citizens of Athens to banish for 10 years anyone they deemed to be a threat—for instance, anyone suspected of planning to seize power. Every year, the Athenian citizens voted in the public assembly on whether they considered a political banishment was necessary, and if the answer was yes, a quorum of 6,000 citizens assembled at a later date. Each of these citizens had to scratch the name of the political leader he wanted banished on a potsherd (a fragment of broken pottery). Whoever received the most votes had to leave the city for 10 years. The potsherd on which a vote was recorded was called an ostracon, hence the term *ostracism*.

## Democracy in practice

The system of government in Athens was a direct democracy. The most important element of government was the *ecclesia*, which was a general assembly of all citizens. Other administrative bodies were composed of either the entire citizenry or a number of representatives, who were sometimes elected but were usually appointed by lot.

Most of the important political decisions were made by the *ecclesia*, which in the fifth century BCE met around 10 or 11 times a year. Extra meetings could be convened if exceptional circumstances

The Council consisted of 10 groups, each with 50 men, selected annually by a complex system that ensured each of the 10 groups represented the total polis. The same principle was applied to the hoplite army, which was also split into 10 subdivisions. The intention behind this system was to avoid a situation where all the citizens living in a particular region could join together to form a section of the Council or a division of the army. A scenario like that might have allowed the most powerful aristocrats in a given region to gain political or military control of Athens.

Under the new system, the entire Athenian citizenry was split into 10 sections, called *phylae*, with each section representing the polis in miniature. To form the *phylae*, the local communities in Attica were divided into 10 urban, 10 made it necessary. However, the agenda for meetings of the *ecclesia* was set by the Council of 500, which therefore exerted a great influence on the assembly. Apart from subjects such as the grain supply, military affairs, and the appointment of magistrates—all of which had to be addressed—the Council determined what would be dealt with at each meeting. The public assembly could accept the Council's agenda but could also add alternative suggestions or new items for discussion. Because the public assembly had the last word, a powerful Council did not necessarily pose a threat to the Athenian democracy.

The preliminary work that was necessary for the Council to draw up the agenda took a great deal of time. Discussions within the smaller body of the Council were more efficient than consulting with the several thousand members of the public assembly. For this reason, the assembly was prepared to delegate less important matters and emergency decisions to the Council.

## Membership of the Council

Members of the Council were citizens and 30 years of age or older. They held the position for a period of one year and never served more than twice in a lifetime. The Council members were drawn from all over Attica—50 men from each of the 10 *phylae*. Within each *phyle*, Council members were chosen by lot from a pool of candidates supplied by all the villages and urban districts. In the small communities, every adult male probably had a chance to serve on the Council at least once, which was less likely in the larger communities.

The Council met frequently but was not in permanent session. One of its tasks was to carry out the decisions made by the public assembly. Since this task required an administration that was available all the time, the *prytane* system was created. The *prytane* was a kind of permanent committee of Council members. Each of the 50-man groups taken from the 10 *phylae* served for one of the 10 months of the Athenian year.

*This ancient Greek relief depicts athletes training.*

The daily administration was formed by the 50 men of the *prytane*. A smaller group selected from the 50 was ready and available 24 hours a day, living together for this purpose in a building on the agora, the open space where the public assembly was sometimes held. The *prytanes* prepared, convened, and recessed meetings of the Council and the assembly and received envoys, messengers, complaints, and a wide range of requests. Because the Greeks liked to introduce a competitive element into everything they did, the various *prytanes* competed for the title of "best *prytane* of the year."

Every 24 hours, the *prytane* had a different chairman, also appointed by lot. A man could hold this chairmanship only once in his lifetime, but an ordinary man from a small village in Attica had a good chance of becoming chairman of the daily administration, an indication that direct democracy really worked.

Each village had to supply a number of Council members each year, and because the number of men who were 30 years of age and older was limited, it was highly probable that every eligible male would be selected at least once. Once chosen, he would belong to the *prytane* administration for a month, and with 35 or 36 days in the Athenian month, he would have a 70 percent chance of being appointed chairman.

*Black-figure pottery such as this illustrated vase first emerged in the seventh century BCE.*

In the fifth century BCE, the chairman of the *prytane* also acted as chairman of the Council and the public assembly if those bodies happened to meet on that day. He was also in charge of the city seal and the keys to the temples, which also functioned as the city's treasury. These were heavy responsibilities for a farmer from a small village.

## Limitations

Athenian democracy had several limitations. All citizens were allowed to participate in direct democracy, regardless of their descent and the amount of property they owned, but not everyone living in the polis was a citizen. First of all, women were excluded. This is not surprising; women were excluded from almost all public life in Greece. Although nominally citizens (if born to citizens), women were considered apolitical beings and had virtually no civil rights.

Other criteria for entitlement to citizenship included being free (slaves had no civil rights whatsoever), being of Athenian descent (immigrants who settled in Attica could not become citizens), and being an adult. Relatively few men were full Athenian citizens; democracy was intended for a small minority of the population.

Also, even though there were tens of thousands of citizens from all over Attica who were eligible to attend the public assembly, it seems unlikely that very many did so. Although it was their right, it was not their obligation. Many lived too far away or were simply unable or unwilling to miss a day's work. Because of these factors, it seems probable that only a minority of the citizens actually attended the assembly, even when important issues were being discussed. Indeed, there was only enough room for around 6,000 men on the Pnyx, the hill in Athens where the assembly usually convened after the end of the sixth century BCE. Although 6,000 men represented only a small proportion of those who were eligible to vote, it was apparently still considered enough to be termed the "entire population of Athens."

However, thanks to Cleisthenes's reforms, a participatory democracy—at least in theory—had been created in Athens by the end of the sixth century BCE. Whether or not they did so, all citizens had the right to participate collectively in the government of the polis.

## A threat from the east

As the sixth century BCE drew to a close, a new danger threatened the young Athenian democracy. The Persians in the east were looking to Anatolia to expand their immense empire. Under their king Cambyses II, the Persians had already annexed the Ionian cities on the Anatolian west coast, thereby extending Persian rule from the Indus River right to the Aegean Sea. It was looking increasingly likely that the Persians would try to subdue the small city-states of mainland Greece, which was now on the frontier of the Persian Empire.

**See also:**

The Persian Wars (volume 3, page 326) • Sparta and Athens (volume 2, page 258)

*The Erechtheion, a temple found on the Acropolis in Athens, was built in the fourth century BCE.*

# GREEK RELIGION

The ancient Greeks worshipped a wide array of gods, many of whom were believed to dwell on Mount Olympus. Worship was usually carried out openly, although more secretive mystery cults were also popular.

Greek religion was polytheistic in nature, meaning that it involved the worship of many gods. The Greeks believed that these deities had a profound influence on life on earth. Most of the gods were believed to have human form and, although they were immortal, they had many mortal defects, being prey to lust, jealousy, anger, and other human failings. In order to propitiate a god, the Greeks offered prayers, sacrifices, and public festivals to win divine approval and help in their human endeavors.

## The first Greek gods

The origins of the Greeks' religion lie far back in antiquity. When the first Indo-European tribes reached mainland Greece around 2000 BCE, they brought with them a warlike religion presided over by a patriarchal god. This deity was a universal divine father figure worshipped by Indo-European peoples from India to western Europe. The Greeks knew him as Zeus, the king of the gods who lived on Mount Olympus (see box, page 314). Other deities of Indo-European heritage were Helios, the sun god, and Eos Aurora, the goddess of dawn.

In Minoan Crete, many female deities were worshipped, and they may have been adapted later by the mainland Greeks. The Linear B tablets from the Mycenaean era (c. 1600–1250 BCE) mention several gods who are later found in the Greek pantheon, such as Zeus, Hera, Dionysus, and Hermes. It is certain that by the time of Archaic Greece (c. 750–500 BCE) multiple influences had contributed to the family of Greek gods; often, they would become merged with similar deities from neighboring regions, a process known as syncretism.

One Greek god whose characteristics were derived from a variety of sources was Apollo. He was the main god of the Dorian people, who invaded mainland Greece around 1250 BCE after the collapse of the Mycenaean civilization. As well as being a sun deity, Apollo was also the god of music and dance. In this aspect of his personality, he may have had Minoan antecedents. Apollo the archer, the god who brought disease with his arrows, may have had Semitic or Hittite connections. In some cases, the influences from the east were very strong. The Greek goddess of love, Aphrodite, shared many similarities with the Phoenician deity Astarte, who in turn was closely related to the Babylonian goddess Ishtar.

In addition to the chief gods and goddesses, the Greeks recognized the existence of heroes (including demigods, or deified mortals) and spirits of various kinds, both good and evil. Greek myths also featured a number of odd creatures that combined the characteristics of different animals. Many were associated with Dionysus, the popular god of wine and pleasure. These creatures included satyrs, which had the legs of a goat or horse and the upper body of a man, and centaurs, which had the head and torso of a man and the body of a horse. There were also various types of nymphs, which were beautiful female spirits associated with natural features such as trees, rivers, and springs.

## The temples

Each god had his or her own temple, and one god might have many temples spread throughout Greece. An image of the god was kept in the temple, which at first was a simple wooden construction but was later made of stone. These stone temples were larger than the earlier ones and were surrounded by a colonnade. In the center was a small chamber in which the idol of the god was housed. The temple

*This detail from an Italian fresco depicts the Greek sun god Apollo crossing the sky in his chariot.*

311

*This silver coin from around 200 BCE bears the features of Helios, a Greek sun god. Helios predated the better-known sun god Apollo.*

Sacrifices were considered the most important element of worship. They were performed before battles, after planting crops, or before any risky enterprise. The object was to placate a god and enlist help. The most usual sacrifice was that of an animal, generally a sheep or goat, which was ritually killed to make an offering of blood to the god. After the animal was sacrificed, it was sometimes totally cremated. However, a god was more often considered to be satisfied with just the aroma of the cremated shanks, and the other meat was eaten during the feast that followed the offering.

Non-blood offerings included the placing or burning of food on the altar, libations (pourings) of wine, milk, olive oil, or aromatics, and the burning of incense. People made these sacrifices in order to express gratitude or to honor a god, or because they sought something from a deity in return. Worshippers often asked a god to give them something first, vowing to bring an offering if the god complied with the request. Offerings made in fulfilment of such a vow included land, slaves, cattle, money, and valuables such as weapons, textiles, jewelry, or objects of art.

## Priesthood

Most temples had their own priests or priestesses, but it was not necessary for a member of the priesthood to attend a sacrifice. Priests had no special status, and priests and priestesses were often chosen or drawn by lot to serve for a set period of time. The gods were worshipped at home as well as in public. Every home had altars to the various household gods, such as Hestia, the goddess of the hearth.

also had an altar, which was usually situated outside at the front. The altar was used for sacrifices.

Greek religious life featured a number of rituals and celebrations, which were carried out throughout the year and were often shared by the entire community. Each city had its own patron god or goddess—Athena was the goddess of Athens, for example—with temples dedicated to him or her. The patron was honored with prayers, sacrifices, processions, and festivals of song, dance, poetry, drama, and athletics.

## Sacrifices

The Greeks believed that the gods represented vast forces of nature before which humans were helpless and insignificant. However, people could try to influence the actions of the gods through prayer and sacrificial offerings.

## RELIGION IN LITERATURE

Two Greek writers in particular provide insights into Greek religion. One of these is Homer, who lived in the ninth or eighth century BCE. In his great poems the *Iliad* and the *Odyssey*, Homer gives a vivid picture of a Greek society in which the gods play a vital part. He is also credited with the authorship of the *Homeric Hymns*, poetic celebrations of the many Greek gods.

Another important writer is the poet Hesiod, who lived around 700 BCE. In his *Theogony*, or *Birth of the Gods*, Hesiod compiled a vast collection of Greek myths and described deities that were not mentioned by Homer. Hesiod also described the creation of the world, the origins of the gods, and related many anecdotes about the gods.

## Oracles

In order to gain answers to specific questions, the Greeks consulted oracles. An oracle was a medium who could make a response on behalf of a god. From the eighth century BCE onward, certain sanctuaries associated with oracles became widely honored. Priests, who were sometimes local officials, were present at each of these sites to offer an interpretation of the oracle or prophecy. However, the priests did not have any particular training and were not considered to have any unusual powers. One of the earliest oracles, mentioned in Homer's *Iliad*, was that of Zeus in Dodona, in northern Greece.

The most famous oracle of the ancient Greek world was the one at Delphi, on the top of Mount Parnassus. Suppliants flocked there to put questions to Apollo through the medium of his special priestess, the Pythia. Questions could involve anything from trivial personal matters to important affairs of state. The Pythia fell into a trance in order to give Apollo's answers, which were famous for their vague and confusing

*This ancient Greek vase painting depicts two men performing a sacrifice.*

313

# THE GODS OF OLYMPUS

The highest mountain in mainland Greece, Mount Olympus, was thought to be the home of the 12 most important gods, who all belonged to the same family. These gods were presided over by Zeus. The others in the Olympian family were Hera, Poseidon, Athena, Apollo, Artemis, Aphrodite, Hermes, Demeter, Dionysus, Hephaestus, and Ares.

As king of the gods, Zeus ruled the skies. He was also a lord of justice and a peacemaker. He had two brothers. One of them, Poseidon, was lord of the waters, while the other brother, Hades, was lord of the underworld and did not belong on Olympus. Hera, both the sister and wife of Zeus, was the goddess of women and marriage. She and Zeus were the parents of Ares and Hephaestus.

Athena was the daughter of Zeus alone—she was born, fully grown, out of his head. Athena was an important goddess, the patron goddess of the city of Athens. She was a virgin and a goddess of war. She was also the protector of women's handicrafts. Apollo and Artemis were the twin children of Zeus by the demigoddess Leto. Apollo, usually depicted as a handsome young man carrying a lyre, was the god of music and poetry and was the leader of the nine Muses. He was also the god of medicine and of oracles. Artemis, another virgin goddess, ruled over hunting, the wilderness, and wild animals.

Aphrodite, the goddess of love and sexuality, was born from the sea. Hermes, the son of Zeus and the demigoddess Maia, was the messenger of the gods and the protector of shepherds, travelers, and heralds. He also guided the souls of the dead to the underworld. The mysterious Demeter, the sister of Zeus, Poseidon, and Hades, was the goddess of agriculture and fertility. She was the mother of Persephone, who was carried away by Hades to the underworld.

Another very important god, Dionysus, was the son of Zeus and the Theban princess Semele. He was the god of wine and ecstasy, and his festivals were very popular with the common people of Greece. Dionysus was, however, also the god of madness and death. Hephaestus, a son of Zeus and Hera, was the smith-god, the patron of all craftsmen. Married to Aphrodite, Hephaestus was considered the outsider of the Olympian family and was always depicted as a cripple.

Ares, also a son of Zeus and Hera, was the god of war and was often Athena's adversary. In myth, Ares was Aphrodite's lover, and one story relates how he killed another of her lovers, Adonis, in a fit of jealousy.

*The Ares Borghese, made around the second century CE, is one of the most famous depictions of the Greek war god.*

nature. Priests were on hand to transcribe the oracle's pronouncements. In fact, one of the first uses of writing in Greece was to record oracular utterances. Many of the sayings of the oracles, at Delphi and elsewhere, were written down to support certain policies.

Divination was another way of finding answers to questions. Seers were practiced in the interpretation of dreams, of the flights of birds, of the spirals of smoke rising from an altar, and of the arrangement of the entrails of a newly sacrificed animal.

## The mysteries

Between the seventh and sixth centuries BCE, mystery religions began to flourish. While the usual religious observances of the polis community were very public,

the mysteries consisted of closely guarded rituals that were only open to worshippers who had been inducted into a secret cult. The purpose of the mysteries was to liberate the initiates from their earthly bonds and to show them the way to a happy life in another world after death. The secrets of the rituals were so closely guarded that there is no way to know what took place in them.

The most famous Greek mysteries were those held in the town of Eleusis, northwest of Athens. For a thousand years, between around 600 BCE and 400 CE, people gathered there to become initiates. The subject of the Eleusian mysteries was the legend of the goddess Persephone, who was abducted by her uncle, Hades, and taken to the underworld. Her disappearance so traumatized her mother, the

*The Temple of Poseidon at Cape Sounion is one of the most imposing of the surviving Greek temples.*

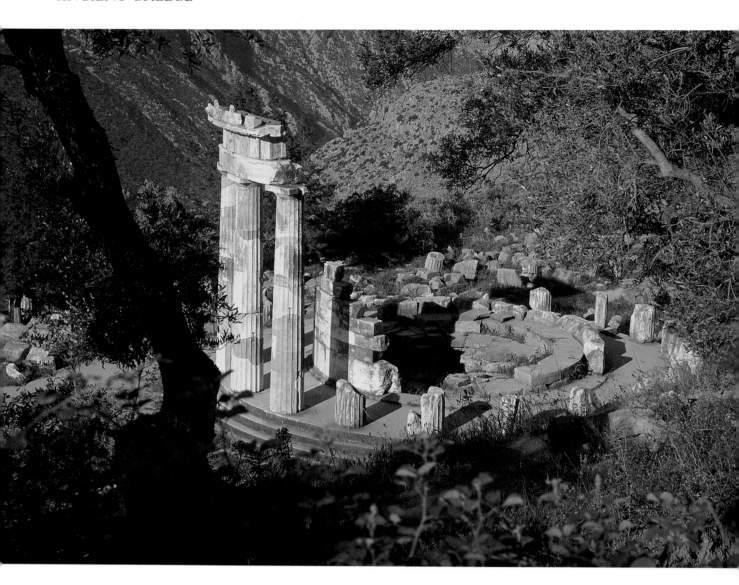

*The Sanctuary of Athena Pronaia is found at Delphi, which is more often associated with the worship of the god Apollo.*

agriculture goddess Demeter, that the crops ceased to grow. Eventually, an agreement was made that allowed Persephone to spend part of the year with her mother and part in the underworld. The legend was used to explain the seasons.

The initiation ceremonies took place every year on the same date during the autumn. The main public event was a procession from Athens to Eleusis covering some 25 miles (40 km) over the "Holy Road." Then, in a secret ceremony held in Demeter's temple, the initiates underwent the secret rites that admitted them to the mysteries. Those who attended this ceremony had to swear an oath of secrecy, and they left the temple with the expectation of a better life in the hereafter.

## The first atheists

Most Greeks took part in community rituals, believed in the supernatural powers of the gods, consulted an oracle occasionally, and possibly were initiated into a mystery cult. However, not everyone could accept all the ideas that were inherent in Greek religion. In particular, the notion that the gods could assume many forms troubled some people. The image of Aphrodite, for example, took different forms in different city-states. In addition, the fact that good was not always rewarded and that evil was not always punished was an important stumbling block for others.

Greek thinkers came up with various theories to address these concerns. One theory was atheism—the idea that there is no god at all. One of the first known atheists was the philosopher Diagoras of Melos, who lived in the fifth century BCE. Diagoras, a stoic and a student of the philosopher Democritus, apparently came up with his theory out of anger at the fact that the gods did not punish wrongdoing—possibly because they did not act against the Athenians, who had slaughtered the citizens of his native city. Diagoras is said to have ridiculed the gods on a number of occasions, most notably when he cut up a statue of the demigod Heracles to provide enough firewood to cook turnips.

**See also:**

The Great Philosophers (volume 3, page 352)

*Persephone and Hades are shown seated on their thrones in the underworld in this Greek relief sculpture. The story of Persephone was central to several mystery cults.*

# THE BIRTH OF DRAMA

One of the most important cultural developments to occur in Greece in the sixth and fifth centuries BCE was the growth of drama. Originally part of religious festivals, plays gradually became art forms in their own right.

## TIME LINE

**c. 550 BCE**

Thespis, first known playwright, active around this time.

**c. 535 BCE**

Great Dionysian festival held for first time in Athens; part of festivities is competition between playwrights.

**468 BCE**

Sophocles takes part in his first Dionysian festival; he wins competition.

**458 BCE**

*Oresteia* trilogy by Aeschylus wins competition at Dionysian festival.

**431 BCE**

Euripides' great tragic play *Medea* performed for first time.

**427 BCE**

*Revellers*, debut play by comic dramatist Aristophanes, first produced.

The drama, and ultimately the theater, grew out of annual festivals held in honor of the god Dionysus, who was the god of wine, intoxication, and ecstasy, a word that implied a way of losing yourself in an alcohol-induced frenzy and becoming one with the god. Dionysus was also regarded as the god of reproduction and of the life force of all living beings. However, because ecstasy also implied a loss of self-control leading to insanity, another view of Dionysus was that he was the god of confusion, destruction, and death. For this reason, he was considered to be the god of the whole of life in all its aspects.

## Festivals

Festivals held in honor of Dionysus involved processions of devotees wearing masks and dancing and singing. This type of procession of ordinary citizens was called a *comos* and was usually quite riotous. The words sung by the *comos* revelers were generally satirical and probably involved repartee with onlookers. Comedy seems to have developed from this exchange of backchat.

Tragedy had a different origin. At more solemn festivals for Dionysus a chorus would chant or sing a narrative poem called a *dithyramb*, which told the story of a Greek myth. In time, the leader of the chorus began to step out from the chorus and assume the role of a character in the myth. The person generally credited with this innovation was the chorus master and poet Thespis, who is thought in the sixth century BCE to have introduced an actor wearing a mask to speak lines in between chanting from the chorus. The poet-dramatist Aeschylus (525–456 BCE) later introduced a second actor, which laid the foundation for the development of "drama."

Thespis was a writer, composer, choreographer, director, and actor all in one. Such a person was known as a *tragoidos* (goat bard), probably because the *tragoidoi* took part in a competition that awarded a goat as the prize. The word *tragedy* is supposedly derived from *tragoidos*.

In the middle of the sixth century BCE, performances of tragedy and competitions among poets were the heart of the newly established great Dionysian festival, held every spring in Athens. Each year, a wooden stage and wooden stands for spectators were set up in the agora (the public square where the assembly was held), but one year in the fifth century BCE, the stands collapsed. The accident resulted in the building of a new theater on the south slope of the

*Greek drama had its origins in festivals held to honor the god Dionysus, depicted here in a Greek vase illustration.*

318

Acropolis, close to an existing shrine to Dionysus. This theater consisted of a natural auditorium formed by the curve of the hillside and overlooking a circular orchestra at the base of the hill. The orchestra was where the chorus and the actors performed. This plan was followed by all later Greek theaters.

The festival lasted for five days and five nights. On the first day, there was a great procession, and offerings were brought to Dionysus. This was followed by a *dithyramb* competition, an impressive spectacle with 10 boys' choruses and 10 men's choruses of 50 singers each. The day closed with a *comos* procession, usually involving a masquerade and plenty of rough merrymaking.

On the second day, the dramas began, and five comedies by five different authors were performed. Each of the following three days then featured a *tetralogy*—three tragedies and a satyr play—by a single author. The satyr play featured a chorus of clownish satyrs (creatures that were half goat and half man) and was intended to provide comic relief after a long day of tragedy.

The eight authors chosen to challenge each other for the best comedy and tetralogy at the festival were selected by the *archons* (magistrates). The *archons* then looked for *choregi* (literally "chorus leaders") to act as producers. These *choregi* were wealthy people who were obliged to pay most of the costs of the

**This carving of a Greek theatrical mask dates to the third century BCE.**

event from their own pockets, with the rest being paid for by the state.

After a lengthy pre-festival period of rehearsals, the festival performances were all given. The jury that decided the winners was a committee of 10 people chosen by lot. One *dithyramb* chorus, one comedy, and one *tetralogy* were selected as the winning pieces, and the *choregi* of the winners shared the honors.

## The chorus

Greek theater in the fifth century BCE was dominated by the chorus. Comedies had a chorus of 24, tragedies 12 or 15. The chorus recited or sang the text in unison, emphasizing the words with gestures or dance steps. Dance was an integral part of the drama, and the colorful costumes and masks worn by the actors greatly added to the effect of the plays.

To begin with, both the chorus and the actors were located on the orchestra. As it became obvious that a place was needed for the two, and later three, actors to change their costumes, a hut called a skene was erected at the back of the orchestra. It was quickly realized that the skene could be used as a background to the dramatic action, so the drama might be seen to take place in front of a building, such as a temple or palace, rather than in the open countryside as had been the case previously. Later still, a low platform was built at the rear of the orchestra and in front of the skene. Under this new arrangement, the chorus members were located on the orchestra, while the actors were located on the raised platform to declaim and sing the most important parts of the tragedy.

Unlike the members of the chorus, the actors were professionals. Because no more than three actors were allowed on stage in the tragedies, the actors often had double roles. Women were not allowed to act—although they could be members of the chorus—so female roles were played by men, which was made possible by the use of masks. The actors also changed the timbre of their voices when playing women.

In the fifth century BCE, no pieces were performed twice in Athens, which meant that 17 premieres were enacted every year. Only a very few of these plays have survived in their complete state—just 44 pieces out of the thousand or more that must have been performed.

## The tragic poets

The oldest dramatist-poet known by name is Thespis, but none of his work survives. A little more is known about Choerilus, whose career began at the same time as that of Thespis in the sixth century BCE. His surviving work includes a couple of small fragments and one title, *Alope*, which may have been a satyr play. Another successful dramatist from this time was Phrynichus (c. 540–475 BCE). He was a winner in the poetic competitions held during the last

*The Theater of Dionysus was the largest theater in Athens. Plays by all the great Athenian writers were performed there.*

decade of the sixth century BCE. Perhaps his most interesting work is *The Capture of Miletus*. This tragedy is based on a piece of contemporary history—the story of the siege of the Ionian city of Miletus by the Persians in 494 BCE.

## Aeschylus

The heyday of Greek tragedy began with Aeschylus, who was born in 525 BCE in Eleusis, northwest of Athens. He wrote around 90 plays, all of them destined to be performed at the annual Dionysian festival. Only seven of them have survived, however. One of his main contributions to Greek drama was to write a part for a second actor, which greatly increased the possibility for dramatic confrontations. Most of the plots for his plays were taken from Greek myths and show how the actions of men on earth bring retribution from the gods.

Aeschylus first took part in the competition of the tragedians in the Dionysia of 499 BCE, but he did not win until 484 BCE. Of his seven surviving tragedies, three formed the trilogy with which he won the Dionysian competition in 458 BCE. The *Oresteia* trilogy was probably his last work and is an outstanding example of Aeschylus's poetic style and mastery of suspense.

The *Oresteia* concerns the fate of the royal family of the Atreides. The action of the first play, *Agamemnon*, takes place in the palace of Mycenae, where Clytemnestra awaits the return after many years of her husband Agamemnon, the leader of the Greeks in the Trojan War. Clytemnestra hates her husband, who sacrificed their daughter Iphigenia to appease the gods. During his absence, Clytemnestra has had an affair with Aegisthus and now, when Agamemnon returns, they plot to kill him. In spite of being warned of his danger by Cassandra, the Trojan princess whom Agamemnon has brought with him from Troy as a slave, Agamemnon is murdered by the lovers soon after his arrival.

*This 19th-century-CE drawing depicts the killing of Agamemnon and Cassandra by Clytemnestra and her lover Aegisthus. The story of the murder is told in Aeschylus's play Agamemnon.*

In the second drama of the trilogy, *Libation Bearers*, the murder of Agamemnon is avenged by his son Orestes, who kills his own mother and her lover. In the third part, *Eumenides*, Orestes, pursued by the furies (the goddesses of vengeance), finds no peace until a special court in Athens acquits him of the charge of matricide.

Of the four other remaining works of Aeschylus, *Persians* is based on the story of the Greek victory over the Persians at Salamis, told from the Persian point of view. *Suppliants* tells the story of the Danaides, the 50 daughters of Danaus (the king of Libya), who were promised in marriage to the 50 sons of his brother Aegyptus. *Seven Against Thebes* is about the struggle between the brothers Eteocles and Polyneices for possession of the throne of Thebes, and the battle of the Seven Heroes for possession of the city. *Prometheus Bound* portrays the story of the demigod Prometheus, who gave fire to mankind in defiance of Zeus. Zeus punished him by chaining him to a rock, where an eagle tore out his liver every day. In most of Aeschylus's dramas, the main theme is that man must yield to the jealous power of the gods.

## Sophocles

Aeschylus's successor, and for a time his competitor, was Sophocles (c. 496–406 BCE), who was almost 30 years younger than Aeschylus and came from an old, aristocratic Athenian family. As well as being a poet-dramatist, Sophocles served as one of the Athenian *strategoi* (generals) for the year 440 BCE.

Sophocles' literary career began in 468 BCE, when he took part in the Dionysian competition for the first time and defeated Aeschylus. Sophocles won the competition another 18 times. Although Sophocles was the most popular tragedian of Athens, only seven of his estimated 123 tragedies have survived.

David Oyelowo and Hayley Atwell perform in a modern London production of an English-language adaptation of *Prometheus Bound* by Aeschylus.

Sophocles was an innovator. He was the dramatist who first introduced a third actor on the stage, a convention later taken over by Aeschylus. Sophocles also broke with the tradition that the tragedian must act in his own plays, as Aeschylus still did.

Sophocles was less convinced of the implacability of fate than Aeschylus was and laid greater emphasis on individual human will. However, the consequences of trying to alter one's fate could be tragic. In the plays, this possibility leads to heightened dramatic tension.

None of Sophocles' trilogies remain. The seven surviving tragedies are all independent works in their own right— *Ajax*, *Antigone*, *Electra*, *Oedipus Rex*, *Trachiniai*, *Philoctetes*, and *Oedipus at*

**In this 15th-century-CE manuscript illustration, Jocasta kills herself after realizing that she has married her son Oedipus. The story is contained in Oedipus Rex by Sophocles.**

De Jocasta thebarum regina, Capitulum. xxiij.

*Colonus.* Of all the extant Greek tragedies, *Oedipus Rex* is probably the best known. The play shows a great man brought low through ignorance of his origins. Because he has been raised not knowing who his parents are, Oedipus, the king of Thebes, discovers that he has unknowingly killed his father, Laius, and married his mother, Jocasta. When he realizes that he has committed patricide and incest, Oedipus puts out his own eyes in horror and then goes into exile, where he dies.

In *Antigone,* Sophocles examines the conflict between human laws and divine laws. Antigone is the daughter of Oedipus and goes with him into exile. Her brothers Eteocles and Polyneices fight for the vacant throne of Thebes, and both die in battle before the gates of the city. The throne now falls to their uncle, Creon, and he strictly forbids Antigone to bury the body of her brother Polyneices, whom he regards as a traitor to his country. Creon decrees that the body must lie dishonored on the battlefield, a prey to dogs and vultures.

Antigone, however, knows that she has a moral obligation to give her brother a fitting burial, so his spirit will have rest. By disobeying her uncle, Antigone sets in motion a tragic chain of events that leads not only to her own death but also to that of her lover Haemon.

In this play, Sophocles directs all his attention to the conflict within the human soul. Antigone, Haemon, and even Creon are torn between human and divine laws. Because of this emphasis on human psychological dilemmas, *Antigone* is regarded as one of the greatest of all tragedies.

## Euripides

Euripides (c. 485–406 BCE) was the youngest of the three great tragedians. He wrote around 92 plays, of which 18 tragedies and 1 satyr play remain.

Because his characters seem more human and realistic than those of his predecessors, he is seen as the most modern of the Greek tragedians. His play *Medea*, recognized as one of the greatest of the Greek tragedies, tells the story of the enchantress Medea, who helped Jason gain the golden fleece. After the couple settle in Corinth, they have two children, but Jason is unfaithful and threatens to leave Medea. Driven by pathological jealousy, Medea murders her own children as revenge on her husband.

In *Hippolytus*, Euripides paints a sympathetic portrait of a woman in the grip of an obsessive love. To punish the youth Hippolytus, who has angered her, the goddess Aphrodite makes his stepmother Phaedra fall in love with him. When Phaedra declares her love, the chaste youth is horrified. Phaedra commits suicide but leaves a note accusing Hippolytus of lusting after her. When Hippolytus's father, Theseus, hears of this, he banishes his son, at the same time laying a curse on him that swiftly results in his death.

## The comic dramatists

Another group of Greek dramatists wrote comedies, which generally made fun of current politicians and events. The greatest of these dramatists was Aristophanes (c. 450–388 BCE). He was the leading exponent of what is now called Greek "Old Comedy." His first work, entitled *Revellers*, was produced in 427 BCE. That play no longer survives, but of the 30 or so plays he wrote, 11 still do exist.

An enormously popular dramatist in his time, Aristophanes did not hesitate to lampoon leading politicians of the day. His play *Knights*, first performed around 424 BCE, contains a satirical portrait of the ambitious politician Cleon, mocking

his attempts to be elected as a *strategos*. In *Frogs*, meanwhile, Aristophanes ridicules his fellow playwrights Euripides and Aeschylus.

In the late fourth century BCE, "New Comedy" emerged. The leading exponent of this style was Menander (c. 341–291 BCE). In this kind of comedy, there was virtually no satire. The plays dealt with social comedy, showing family situations and highlighting individual characters with their various foibles. This form of drama was to have a great influence on the development of comedy in the Roman era.

*This bust depicts the playwright Euripides. Euripides is seen as one of the three great Athenian tragedians, the other two being Sophocles and Aeschylus.*

**See also:**

The Greek Legacy (volume 3, page 404) • The Peloponnesian War (volume 3, page 368)

# THE PERSIAN WARS

In the fifth century BCE, the two greatest powers of the Mediterranean world—Greece and Persia—were involved in a titanic military struggle. The great battles of the Persian Wars—Thermopylae, Marathon, and Salamis—are famous to this day.

By the end of the sixth century BCE, the Persian Empire was the greatest the world had ever known. Its rise to power came with stunning rapidity. Only 50 years earlier, the Persians had been just one of several small peoples inhabiting the Iranian plain in the Middle East. They were also subjects of the Medes. In 549 BCE, the Persians' ambitious king Cyrus the Great (ruled 559–529 BCE) led a revolt against the Medes and defeated them. By this victory he became lord of one of western Asia's great kingdoms. He then embarked on a campaign of foreign conquests. First in his sights was Lydia in Anatolia, another great power. He marched into Lydia in 546 BCE and took its capital, Sardis. He then annexed the Greek cities in the western part of Anatolia, which was known as Ionia.

Cyrus seized Babylon in 539 BCE, making him lord of the mighty Babylonian Empire. By the end of the century, the Persian dominions stretched from the Aegean Sea in the west to the Indus Valley in the east and from the Danube River in the north to the Red Sea and Persian Gulf in the south.

After the death of Cyrus, his son, Cambyses II (ruled 529–522 BCE), succeeded in adding Egypt to the Persian Empire. Darius I (ruled 521–486 BCE) was anxious to extend his boundaries to the northwest. By 512 BCE, he had crossed the Bosporus and was actively seeking conquests on the west side of the Black Sea all the way to the mouth of the Danube, but with little success. However, Darius did succeed in conquering Thrace and Macedon, which meant that his empire then bordered the northwest extremity of mainland Greece.

Between the eighth and sixth centuries BCE, Sparta and Athens had become the predominant city-states of Greece. With all of mainland Greece feeling threatened by the presence of the mighty Persian Empire on the border, it seemed that maintaining the balance of power between Persia and Greece would depend on the lead of these two cities.

## The Ionian Rebellion

In 499 BCE, a massive rebellion against Persian dominance in Anatolia broke out in the Ionian coastal cities and the neighboring islands. The reasons for the revolt are not clear, but it may be that the Greeks resented the necessity of doing military service in the Persian army (which applied to everyone, of whatever rank), and there was also resentment against the Greek tyrants who served as puppet overlords for the Persians. The rebellion began on Ionian ships that had been engaged in naval operations on behalf of the Persians. Returning home, the seamen and officers mutinied and

*This modern stele commemorates the lives of the 192 Greeks who died at the Battle of Marathon.*

arrested the ships' commanders. The leader of this uprising was Aristogoras of Miletus, who went on to mastermind the whole rebellion.

The Ionian cities rose up and deposed their puppet tyrants, replacing them with democracies. The rebels turned to the city-states of mainland Greece for support. Only Athens and Eritria responded, both sending squadrons of warships. With the help of Athenian and Eritrean land forces, the rebels marched on Sardis, where Artaphernes, the brother of Darius I, ruled as a satrap (provincial governor). The Greeks succeeded in occupying the lower town but could not take the citadel. Lacking clear leadership, the Greeks retreated, and the retreat deteriorated into chaos. Artaphernes managed to catch up with the Greeks before they could reach the cost and inflicted a heavy defeat on them near Ephesus.

Despite its failure, the rebellion had inspired other Greek cities—in Cyprus, the Dardanelles, and Byzantium—to rise against their Persian oppressors. The Persians gathered a large navy and army and campaigned throughout the region to bring the Greeks to heel. In 494 BCE, Greeks and Persians met at sea, off Samos, to fight a naval battle, but most of the Greek ships fled, perhaps encouraged to do so by Persian promises of lenient treatment for those who did not fight. The remaining ships were routed. Darius exacted a terrible vengeance on Miletus, the center of the Greek rebellion. The city was sacked, and its inhabitants were either deported to Persia or sold into slavery. Other cities were punished according to their part in the rebellion. However, the episode set the scene for the First Persian War.

# CROESUS OF LYDIA

Croesus, king of Lydia (ruled 560–546 BCE), reigned over an immensely rich and powerful kingdom in Anatolia. The Greek cities of Ionia were conquered by the Lydians in the mid-sixth century BCE, greatly adding to the Lydians' prosperity, but the real basis of Lydian wealth lay in their thriving trade and industries and in the gold and silver mined in their lands.

The first modern coins, minted by the Lydians around 600 BCE, were fat disks stamped with pictures and their specified worth. Up to this time, most trade had been carried on by way of barter—the direct exchange of merchandise—though in some areas, grains of gold and silver, or bars of gold, silver, or bronze, were used to represent the value of goods.

Under Croesus, Lydia achieved the peak of its wealth. As he expanded his empire, he got richer on the booty he took; the expression "as rich as Croesus" dates from this time. There is a story that when the great Athenian legal reformer and philosopher Solon visited him, Croesus claimed to be the happiest man on earth because of his wealth. Solon reputedly replied (prophetically as it turned out), "Call no man happy before his death." Croesus was captured by Cyrus of Persia in 546 BCE and, according to the Greek historian Herodotus, was burned to death on a funeral pyre.

*This 17th-century-CE painting depicts King Croesus of Lydia displaying his great wealth to the Athenian statesman Solon.*

## THE PERSIAN WARS

**KEY**

| | |
|---|---|
| | Greek states allied against Persia |
| | Greek states remaining neutral |
| | Macedonian kingdom |
| | Persian Empire on ascension of Xerxes |
| ✗ | Major battle |

## The First Persian War

The Ionian rebellion led Darius to make some concessions to the Greeks of Anatolia He relaxed his regime slightly and did not require the cities to take their old tyrants back. However, he was determined to subdue mainland Greece. In 491 BCE, he sent messengers to all the Greek city-states, requiring them to send "earth and water" to him as a sign of submission. All the communities on the mainland and islands complied with this request—except for Sparta and Athens. As a sign of their contempt, the Athenians threw the Persian messengers into the pit for condemned criminals. In Sparta, the messengers were thrown into a well where, they were told, there was water and earth in abundance.

Outraged by the death of his messengers, Darius was ready to listen to two Greek exiles in his court who convinced him that they had a number of sympathizers in Greece. These two exiles were Hippias, the ex-tyrant of Athens, and Demaratus, an ex-king of Sparta. Darius formed a plan to take Athens and put Hippias back in power there, under Persian rule.

In 490 BCE, Darius sent an expedition, directed explicitly against Athens, to Greece. On board the Persian fleet was the aged Hippias, convinced that he could regain his position of power. The fleet set sail from the island of Samos, crossed the Aegean Sea, and landed at Eritria, where the Persian forces sacked the city and deported its citizens.

## The Battle of Marathon

The Persian army, some 20,000 to 25,000 strong, disembarked at the Bay of Marathon, around 25 miles (40 km) east of Athens. The Persians wanted to make contact with the sympathizers of Hippias, who had his home base on that side of Attica. The Athenians sent to Sparta for assistance, but their request came during a religious festival that the Spartans would not leave. As soon as the Athenians learned of the landing at Marathon, however, they sent a force of 10,000 hoplites, who were joined by 1,000 Plataean soldiers.

*This gold Lydian coin was made around 550 BCE.*

armor was heavier and provided more protection than that of the Persians, and the Greek hoplites were a formidable fighting force. There was a standoff for several days, with the two armies backing off to sleep in camp at night. Eventually, the Persians decided to sail around to the other side of Attica and launch an attack from there.

Once the Persian cavalry was embarked, one of the Greek generals, Miltiades, convinced the overall commander of the troops, Callimachus, to launch an attack. The Greek hoplites advanced at a run, engaging the Persian infantry with devastating results. After the two Persian wings were crushed, the Greeks and Plataeans wheeled in from the sides to decimate the center. The Persians fled, and many of them were cut down before they could reach the ships. The Persians left 6,400 soldiers dead on the field, while the Greeks lost only 192 men. It was a resounding victory for the Greeks.

After the unexpected defeat at Marathon, the Persian fleet sailed around Cape Sounion to make a second landing. The Persians planned to march on Athens, which they believed was unprotected. However, the Athenian army quickly returned to the city in a forced march, reaching it within only seven hours. To make matters worse for the Persians, the Spartan army was rapidly approaching Athens. Discouraged, the Persian fleet retreated.

The two armies drew up in battle formation on the plain of Marathon. The Persian forces consisted of archers, spearmen, and cavalry, while the Greeks had only foot soldiers. However, the Greeks'

## THE MARATHON RACE

After the Athenian victory over the Persians at the Battle of Marathon in 490 BCE, a Greek runner was dispatched to run the 25 miles (40 km) to Athens to bring the good news. Upon arrival, he collapsed from exhaustion and died.

Centuries later, this feat inspired the marathon race. When the Olympic Games were revived in Athens in 1896 CE, they included a long-distance foot race of around that distance. It was called the marathon in honor of the unknown runner. The marathon distance was later standardized at 26 miles, 385 yards (42.2 km).

The story of the athlete who ran from Marathon to Athens has often been intertwined with a separate story, told by Herodotus, of another runner, named Pheidippides, who ran from Athens to Sparta on the eve of the war to ask the Spartans for help. Pheidippides would have run 150 miles (241 km) in two days.

## The Second Persian War

The next Persian attack did not come until 10 years later. The delay was caused by Darius's death in 486 BCE. The subsequent domestic disturbances forced his son Xerxes I (ruled 486–465 BCE) to wait until 481 BCE. According to Herodotus, Xerxes was warned by his advisers against the consequences of a new campaign, but the king continued his preparations for what would become the largest military undertaking in history to that date.

Athens had made good use of the 10-year calm. During that time, the city had transformed itself into a naval power. The events of the Ionian rebellion had demonstrated the importance of having a strong fleet. This change of view was largely due to the foresighted statesman Themistocles, who convinced the Athenian assembly to spend the major part of the profits gained from the newly opened silver mines of Laurium on shipbuilding. The number of Athenian triremes (warships; see box, page 339) rose from 70 to 200.

In 481 BCE, when the Persian preparations for war were already under way, a conference of Greek states met in Corinth, probably at Themistocles'

*The waters off the Greek island of Samos, shown here, were the site of a naval battle between the Greeks and the Persians in 494 BCE.*

instigation, to decide on the tactics to be followed. It was decided to proclaim an overall peace to end ongoing internal conflicts. All states would enter into an alliance against Persia, and none was to consider making a separate peace. The property of traitors would be confiscated and given to the sanctuary in Delphi.

## Wooden walls

Despite this friendly gesture, the prophecies of the Delphi oracle were consistently unfavorable. The people of Delphi were so well informed of the formidable Persian war preparations that they dared recommend nothing less than unconditional surrender. The advice of the oracle "to flee to the ends of the earth" was not appreciated by the Athenians. They asked the oracle for less defeatist counsel, and it replied that only "wooden walls" could protect Athens. Themistocles declared that this meant ships; because the ships had already been built, the Athenians were satisfied.

Athens was joined by 30 other Greek states. They decided to meet the Persian attack head on, with Sparta in charge of the entire military operation. The Greek strategy was essentially to avoid battles on the plains, where the Persian superiority in numbers, and in particular their cavalry, would almost certainly overcome smaller Greek forces. Instead, the Greeks planned to try to engage the Persians either in mountain passes or at sea in narrow channels.

On the Persian side, Xerxes was personally in charge of the new expedition. The winter of

481–480 BCE was devoted to preparations in Sardis. The Persian army, the largest that had ever been assembled, was too large to be transported by sea. Equally, the army was too large to live off the land it had to march through, so arrangements had to be made to supply the army with food by sea.

## Into Greece

In the spring of 480 BCE, Xerxes led his army north and crossed the Dardanelles by means of a bridge constructed of boats built by his engineers. He then trekked into Europe, following the coast. A large fleet of warships and freight vessels accompanied the army. They were ordered not to lose sight of each other, since the land army could not function without the fleet.

From Thessaly to central Greece, the main road ran through the pass of Thermopylae, between the sea and the mountains. There the Greeks waited for the Persians, and a historic three-day battle was fought, which the Greeks eventually lost.

At the same time that the Battle of Thermopylae was happening on land, the Greeks engaged with the Persians in a naval battle at Artemisium, in a sea channel only 6 miles (9.7 km) wide. Although the Persian fleet had originally numbered around 600 ships, it had lost a number of them in recent storms, so it did not greatly outnumber the 370 triremes of the Greeks. The Persians had the advantage that many of their ships were in fact Phoenician, sailed by Phoenician crews, who were generally acknowledged at that time to be the best sailors in the world. However, in the confined waters at Artemisium, superior

*This relief depicts Darius I, the king of Persia at the time of the outbreak of the Persian Wars. Darius insisted that the Greek states should recognize his sovereignty.*

*This 17th-century-CE engraving depicts the Battle of Marathon, one of the key battles of the Persian Wars.*

sailing tactics did not count for much. The Persians' technique was to bring their ships alongside the Greek ships, so that infantrymen could board the enemy ships. The Greeks had their own soldiers aboard their vessels and fought back vigorously. The two fleets inflicted substantial damage on each other, and although the battle was nominally a victory for the Persians, the fact that they had performed so well was a great morale booster for the Greeks. On receiving the news of the defeat at Thermopylae, the Greek ships sailed south.

## Campaign in Attica

Following the battles at Marathon and Artemisium, central Greece and Attica lay open to the advancing enemy. On

## THE BATTLE OF THERMOPYLAE

The pass at Thermopylae was an obvious place for the Greeks to intercept the Persians. It was hemmed in on one side by tall cliffs and on the other by the sea. A Greek force of 9,000 hoplites, under the command of the Spartan king Leonidas, made camp in the pass to await the Persians.

The 200,000 strong Persian army poured into the pass, but because it was so narrow, only a few could engage with the Greeks at a time. The superior equipment of the Greek hoplites gave them a crucial advantage and they were able to hold the pass for two days. On the third day, a local Greek guide treacherously showed the Persians a mountain path that enabled them to come down behind the Greek lines. Realizing that he was outflanked, Leonidas ordered most of his army to retreat south, and with 300 Spartans and around 1,000 other troops, he made a heroic last stand. The Persians attacked, and the Spartans were all killed.

Themistocles' advice, the population of Athens was evacuated to Salamis, an island in the Gulf of Aegina, and the Peloponnese. This proved to be a wise decision, because Xerxes entered Athens and sacked it. From Salamis, Themistocles was forced to watch the clouds of smoke billowing up from the burning temples on the Acropolis.

## The Battle of Salamis

Meanwhile, the Persian fleet had sailed south to Salamis, where the Greek fleet was waiting. According to the poet Aeschylus, who took part in the ensuing battle, the Persian fleet made such an impression that the Spartan leaders were all for retreating from the bay, assembling all land and naval forces by the isthmus of Corinth, and building a wall to block the Persians. Themistocles pointed out that a wall would be useless if the Persian fleet could sail past it. Only "wooden walls" could help.

Before the battle began, Themistocles sent a messenger to Xerxes with false information, claiming that there was dissension among the Greeks, that the Athenians wanted to defect to the enemy, and that the Persians should attack right away if they wanted to take advantage of the situation. The Persians were so confident of victory that Xerxes had a golden throne built on a hill overlooking the harbor of Salamis so he could witness the destruction of the Greek fleet in comfort.

The ruse worked. The Persians, confident that victory would be theirs, sailed into the Salamis narrows by night with the intention of launching an attack at dawn, but first light brought an unwelcome sight. The Greek fleet was drawn up in a semicircular formation, spanning the width of the channel and forming a trap in which the Persian ships were caught. In the ensuing battle, the Greek ships rammed their Persian counterparts, which could not maneuver in the tight situation and, because they were lighter than the Greek triremes, were susceptible to this form of attack. The Persian ships

*This 14th-century-CE manuscript illustration depicts the Battle of Salamis, fought between the Greeks and the Persians.*

# THE HISTORIAN HERODOTUS

The most important source for the history of the Persian Wars is the historian Herodotus, who was born some time around 480 BCE in the Greek city of Halicarnassus in Anatolia. His date of death is also unknown but probably lies sometime between 430 and 420 BCE. Cicero, the Roman statesman and philosopher (106–46 BCE), called Herodotus the father of historiography, that is, the writing of history based on a critical examination of sources. Herodotus attempted to interpret the past, putting a human face on it and infusing it with a moral understanding.

According to Herodotus, his work was the fruit of research and inquiry. He opened his *History*, his account of the Persian Wars, with the following words: "Here follows an explanation of the study that Herodotus of Halicarnassus initiated with the intention that the deeds of the people not be forgotten in time and that the important and amazing feats of the Greeks and non-Greeks be given their due glory, and also to shed light on the reason why they entered into conflict with one another."

Herodotus's *History* is now divided into nine separate books. It does not just tell the story of the Persian Wars themselves; it also attempts to place them into context by giving a history of the Persian Empire. Herodotus's work was based largely on information gathered on his travels throughout Anatolia, Egypt, Palestine, Phoenicia, Mesopotamia, and the Black Sea region. His goal was to collect information, separating what he had seen and heard from other observations. Nevertheless, his work is far from being a dry, historical account. He wrote in an easygoing, engaging style and mixed his accounts of the wars with gossip, descriptions of the personalities involved, and stories of the gods.

*This bust from the fourth century BCE is of Herodotus, the "father of historiography."*

335

capsized, littering the sea with wrecks and corpses. By evening, Xerxes could see that his fleet was crushed.

## Xerxes returns to Asia

Alarmed by the destruction of his fleet, Xerxes began the long march back to Asia with the bulk of his land forces. However, he left a formidable force of around 60,000 men behind under the command of his brother-in-law Mardonius with instructions to continue the planned subjugation of Greece.

Mardonius spent the winter in Thessaly. In the spring, he sent a delegation to Athens offering to repair all the damage and help in reconstructing the city. He hoped by this means to negotiate a settlement with the Athenians excluding Sparta. All he asked in exchange was that Athens should recognize the sovereignty of the Persian king. The Athenians rejected Mardonius's proposals and hastened to reassure the concerned Spartans that they would stand firm for "the Greek brotherhood, the collective ancestry and language, the altars and the sacrifices in which all Greeks share," as Herodotus put it.

Mardonius responded by ravaging Attica and capturing Athens, but he pulled back his troops when the Spartan main force advanced northward. The Greek forces assembled en masse on the plain of Plataea (a few miles south of Thebes) where the Persian army awaited them. The Battle of Plataea ended in a comprehensive victory for the Greek forces and the death of Mardonius. The Persian hopes of conquering Greece were finally at an end.

Meanwhile, reputedly on the same day that the Battle of Plataea was being fought, another encounter took place that completed the Persians' humiliation at the hands of the Greeks. This battle took place at Cape Mycale in Ionia. Some 4,000 Greek hoplites, under the

overall command of the Spartan king Leotychides, landed and confronted a Persian army twice their number. However, the Persian force contained a large contingent of troops from the Greek cities of Lydia. Once the fighting started, a number of the Lydian troops

*This vase painting depicts Greek hoplites with prisoners of war.*

# THE BATTLE OF PLATAEA

On the plain of Plataea in the summer of 479 BCE, a Greek army under the command of Pausanius, the Spartan regent, faced a Persian force under Mardonius. Pausanius had 38,000 heavily armed hoplites from Sparta, Athens, and Corinth, with perhaps an equal number of lightly armed soldiers, but he had no mounted troops. The Persians had the advantage of their formidable cavalry, whose technique against infantry was to charge them, release a hail of javelins and arrows, and then wheel away.

The two armies faced each other across the Asopus River for almost two weeks, with a little daily skirmishing. Each general was reluctant to initiate an attack. Finally, with no access to fresh water, Pausanius decided to withdraw to Plataea. When he saw the Greeks on the move, Mardonius ordered his troops forward to attack.

In the retreat, the Greeks had become separated into several units. One of these units consisted of around 12,000 Spartan hoplites, while another was made up of 8,000 Athenians. At the time of the Persian attack, these units were separated by around 1 mile (1.6 km), so the ensuing battle really took place on two separate fronts. The Spartans turned and formed up in battle order to face the onslaught of the Persian infantry, who were equipped with bows and arrows. Many of the Spartans fell under the rain of arrows, but when the command came to charge, the hoplites proved their superior fighting prowess. In the ensuing chaos, Mardonius was killed, and once their general was dead, the Persians fled. On the other side of the field, the Athenians were engaged with other Persian forces, but once the Persians saw their comrades fleeing, they also ran away. The battle was a resounding victory for the Greeks.

*An undated modern illustration shows the Greek and Persian troops fighting at the Battle of Plataea in 479 BCE.*

*This relief sculpture from the Persian capital of Persepolis dates to the reign of Xerxes I.*

changed sides. Leotychides managed to inflict a decisive defeat on the Persian land forces and captured the Persian fleet, which was moored nearby.

## The end of the war

Even though the battles of Plataea and Cape Mycale effectively ended the danger that the Persians posed to the Greek mainland, sporadic fighting continued for another 30 years. From this time on, it was the Greeks who were on the offensive. The Athenians attempted to secure a complete dominance of eastern Mediterranean trade by systematically driving the Persians out of Ionia and Cyprus. Eventually, in 449 BCE, a peace treaty was negotiated between Persia and Athens, and the Persian Wars were finally at an end.

*This seal depicts the type of Greek warship that would have been used at Salamis.*

**See also:**

The Persians (volume 2, page 232)

## THE GREEK TRIREME

The main type of warship used by the Greeks during the Persian Wars was the trireme (known to the Greeks as a *trieres*). The triremes derived their name from the fact that they were powered by oarsmen arranged in three separate banks, one above the other. This arrangement came about as the solution to the problem of how to fit as many rowers into a ship as possible. The triple-deck system meant that around 170 oarsmen could be fitted into a ship (as well as a number of foot soldiers). Although triremes also used sails, they were lowered before the ships went into battle; the use of oars gave the ships greater maneuverability.

During a naval engagement, a commander could adopt two different tactics. The ship could try to pull up alongside the adversaries, enabling Greek troops to board the enemy vessel and capture it. Alternatively, a ship could simply try to ram the enemy with the prow, which was specially designed for that purpose. In order to execute this maneuver, one fleet had to outflank the other so the prows of at least some of the ships faced the sides of the enemy vessels. This technique was known as the *periplus*. Various defensive formations could be adopted to offer protection. One was the *kyklos*, which was a simple defensive circle where all of the ships had their prows facing outward.

Greek triremes used ramming tactics to win victory in arguably the most famous naval battle of ancient times—Salamis. The Greek fleet was heavily outnumbered, but the quicker and more maneuverable Greek triremes managed to inflict huge damage in the narrow channel where the battle was fought.

# THE AGE OF PERICLES

**D**uring the fifth century BCE, the city of Athens was involved in wars against two major adversaries—Persia and the fellow Greek city of Sparta. However, the period was also a time when democracy and culture flourished.

The Athenian statesman Pericles, who lived from around 495 to 429 BCE, was so important to the development of Athens that historians call the time he was in power the Age of Pericles. Under his guidance, Athens reached the pinnacle of its influence. The city also became an unparalleled center of culture and learning, a process that culminated in the construction of the Parthenon on the Acropolis.

The Athenians enjoyed a good life under Pericles, as he himself described it in a speech: "We have feasts and ceremonies throughout the year. Life is pleasant in our homes, and with our noble behavior, we provide ourselves with pleasures that hinder sadness. The fame of our city brings us fruits from the entire Earth, so we can enjoy foreign and exotic products… We are admirers of beauty, but we remain simple."

## The upbringing of Pericles

Pericles was the son of Xanthippus, a general who led the Athenian contingent that contributed to the defeat of the Persians at Cape Mycale in 479 BCE. Although he came from an aristocratic family, Pericles made his name in politics as a reformer with left-wing leanings. With the support of the common people, he became leader of the popular party. He was a persuasive orator, and when he spoke in the assembly, he could generally convince his listeners of the merit of his proposals. By 460 BCE, he had virtually become head of state.

The Battle of Salamis, where the Greeks routed the Persians in a sea battle in 480 BCE, marked the beginning of the rise of Athenian sea power. After the final defeat of the Persians at Plataea the following year, Athens emerged as the predominant city-state in Greece.

Up until this time, Sparta had been the greatest military power in Greece. At the end of the wars with Persia, however, the Spartans opted for isolation. They returned to their austere lifestyle on the Peloponnese peninsula, where their lands had remained untouched by the Persian Wars. Although they had ample ability and resources to establish military sovereignty throughout Greece, they preferred to concentrate on domestic affairs.

Athens suffered heavily in the wars with Persia, and it remained fearful of a new invasion. To reduce this threat, the Athenians pursued a policy of offensive, expansionist action. After the battles of Salamis and Cape Mycale, the Athenians had undisputed sea supremacy in the eastern Mediterranean region. However, maintaining a large fleet put a severe strain on the funds of Attica, so Athens needed to form alliances to continue military offensives against Persia.

*This bust, created in the second century BCE, is believed to depict the Athenian statesman Pericles, who dominated the politics of Athens for more than 30 years.*

## The Delian League

In 477 BCE, Athens and most of the Aegean city-states formed an alliance against Persia called the Delian League. It was named for the island of Delos, where the meetings of the league were to be held and the funds of the alliance were to be kept. Athens headed the league, but all the members had an equal vote, in principle at least. As the leading member of the league, Athens commanded a fleet of 200 ships, and every ally was required to pay an annual fee to help maintain the fleet. This fee could consist of ships, men, equipment, or silver talents, all assessed according to the resources of the member state.

Between 476 and 466 BCE, a Greek force, under the joint command of generals Cimon and Aristides, succeeded in liberating the coasts of the Aegean from Persian control. One notable success came in 466 when a force led by Cimon destroyed both the Persian fleet and the Persian army near the mouth of the Eurymedon River in Anatolia.

## An Athenian empire

By 466 BCE, most of the members of the league were paying their contributions in silver talents rather than men or goods. This was tantamount to paying tribute. When some of the states started to object, Athens responded ruthlessly. For example, when Naxos objected to paying the tribute and attempted to withdraw from the league, Athens destroyed its forts. Athens then annexed the lands of other recalcitrant allies, distributing the land to its own citizens. The league that had started as a defensive alliance against Persia had become a naval empire run by Athens. It encompassed most of the large islands of the Aegean Sea and many cities to the north, either as equals or as subjected former allies.

Following his famous success at the Eurymedon River, Cimon had become a

*Women draw water from a well in the illustration on this vase from the fifth century BCE.*

treaty with the Persians, which put an end to the Persian Wars. To celebrate the end of hostilities, Pericles embarked on an ambitious building program that resulted in the construction of the group of buildings that are still seen on the Acropolis today. With the Persian threat gone, and Athens obviously in the ascendancy, other city-states on the Greek mainland lined up to join the league. In the long run, however, the result was that the members of the Delian League simply became the vassals of Athens.

## The Peloponnesian War

The Peloponnesian War that was to devastate Greece between the years 431 and 404 BCE was sparked off by growing tension between Athens and the cities of Corinth and Sparta. Corinth had developed from an ancient settlement near the isthmus of Corinth to become a thriving trading city by 1000 BCE. Benefiting from two harbors, one on the Corinthian Gulf and one on the Saronic Gulf, Corinth became the major center of commerce in Greece by 650 BCE. As Athens increased both its naval and commercial activity under Pericles, the older city felt threatened.

The years leading up to 431 BCE also saw relations between Athens and Sparta deteriorate; Sparta saw the growing Delian League as a threat to the stability of the Greek mainland. In 431 BCE, Corinth joined with Sparta in forming the Spartan Confederacy to counteract the rising power of the Delian League. Other members of the confederacy were Thebes, Macedon, and Ambracia on the Ionian coast. These allies faced the might

leading politician. However, his reputation was severely damaged when he took an Athenian contingent to assist Sparta in quelling a slave rebellion. The Athenian expedition ended badly when the Spartans rejected the offer of help. Cimon was ostracized and banished from Athens in 461 BCE. His exit left the stage clear for Pericles to become the city's leading statesman.

In 449 BCE, an Athenian diplomat named Callias succeeded in negotiating a

*The House of the Poseidoniasts stands on the Greek island of Delos. Delos was the meeting place of the Delian League, an association of city-states dominated by Athens.*

of Athens, which was concentrated along the northern and eastern coasts of the Aegean Sea, on most of the large Aegean islands, and in Byzantium. Before long, the rivalry between Sparta and Athens finally erupted into the Peloponnesian War.

In 431 BCE, the Spartans launched the first of a number of raids against the country-side surrounding Athens. As the army of the Spartan Confederacy pillaged unimpeded through the rural regions of Attica, Pericles gathered the residents of Attica inside the city walls of Athens for safety. In the following year, 430 BCE, plague decimated the overcrowded city. The angry and dying Athenians removed Pericles from office, and he was tried and fined for misuse of public funds. After a brief reinstatement, he died in 429 BCE. The Age of Pericles was at an end.

## Golden age of Athens

During the time of Athenian ascendancy under Pericles, the government of Athens and its culture can both be said to have enjoyed a golden age. In particular, the constitution was modified to extend the principles of democracy, further weakening the power of the aristocracy.

The main body of the Athenian political system was the public assembly (the *ecclesia*). In theory, all Athenians could attend the assembly, but in practice, although there were something like 30,000 to 40,000 citizens, only around 6,000 actually attended meetings. The meetings were held around once a month in a natural amphitheater on a

*This statue from the fifth century BCE depicts Athens' patron goddess Athena.*

hillside, where the citizens would debate and vote on motions prepared by the Council in advance. The Council consisted of 500 members who were elected each year, usually from families of the middle and upper classes.

In earlier centuries, one of the most important political offices was that of archon, or magistrate. In 487 BCE, a change had been made in the way the archons were selected. From that point onward, the archons were appointed by lot, rather than elected. The change meant that the magistracy lost much of its importance, as did the Areopagus, the old council of the nobility to which ex-archons belonged. In 462 BCE, the judicial function of the Areopagus was largely taken over by jury tribunals, and its supervision of polis administrators was relegated to the Council of 500.

## Farmers and politicians

Around the middle of the fifth century BCE, it became possible for archons to be drawn from the *zeugitai* (farmers who owned land). A system of attendance fees, payable to magistrates and council and jury members so they did not lose financially because of their services, was introduced. At the beginning of the fourth century BCE, the payment was extended to cover attendance at the public assembly, which meant that all citizens could exercise their political rights without the worry of financial loss. The change was of particular benefit to the *thetes* (small landless farmers and day laborers).

The selection of magistrates by lot carried risks, because some aspects of the role required a degree of specialized knowledge not available to the ordinary man. In an effort to deal with this problem, the Athenians created 10 elected strategoi (commanders-in-chief), who were appointed for one-year terms. They could be reelected but were subject to monitoring by their fellow *strategoi*. If necessary, they could be removed from office by popular vote in the assembly, which meant there was little chance of a *strategos* becoming a tyrant. Pericles served as a *strategos* continuously from 443 to 430 BCE.

## The assembly

Given the size of the assembly, there was only time for a few of those present to speak. Because the issues discussed were often complicated, not everyone could be expected to speak with equal authority. To address several thousand people and convince them to vote the way the speaker wanted demanded special skills in public speaking. In response to these demands, a new class of orator-politicians, called rhetors, developed. These rhetors were generally wealthy people, and they played an essential role in political decision making. Pericles was the most famous of the rhetors, and the most important.

Rhetors spoke either on their own behalf or on behalf of special interest groups. They were not politicians representing specific political parties; political parties did not exist in the modern sense. Athenian democracy allowed everyone, from all classes and walks of life, to participate in political life, but it was not until the second half of the fifth century BCE that nonaristocrats were called on as designated speakers in the public assembly.

*The ruins of the ancient city of Corinth can still be seen to this day. Corinth was a major rival of Athens in the fifth century BCE.*

## Pericles on democracy

A speech attributed to Pericles and believed to have been given around 431 BCE encapsulates his beliefs on the benefits of democracy. The speech praises Athens for its power, strength, prosperity, openness, and freedom, as well as the equality of its citizens. He says: "Our government is no imitation of our neighbors'. On the contrary, we serve as an example for them. We are a democracy, because the government is in the hands of the people and not in the hands of a small group. Our law states that every citizen has equal rights. We Athenians recognize the supremacy of intelligence, and when a fellow citizen distinguishes himself from the others, the people appoint him to the highest positions. This is not the right of a gifted man, but the reward for his great merits. Lack of money is no obstacle to fulfilling high office: any citizen can serve the state. There are no privileges in our political life, nor in our personal relationships; we trust one another."

He goes on to say: "Although there are few among us who are extraordinary enough to formulate proposals, we are all good enough to make decisions. It is our conviction that danger does not lie in discussion, but in ignorance. We have the special characteristic that we can think before we act, even in the middle of action. Others, however, are brave in ignorance, yet hesitate as soon as they begin to think!"

In other parts of the speech, Pericles talks about the glorious history of Athens, the great Athenian Empire, and the courage of Athenian soldiers. He

*This depiction of Artemis, the Greek goddess of hunting, is part of a frieze that decorated the Parthenon in Athens. The Parthenon was a temple to another goddess, Athena. It stood on the Acropolis, the fortified hill at the heart of the city.*

*The Temple of Athena Nike was just one of several magnificent temples erected on the Acropolis in the fifth century BCE.*

paints an ideal picture of Athenian democracy. There is no mention of slavery. Slaves were an accepted fact of life in the Athenian state. Their lack of rights was an issue ignored by all Greeks, including Pericles.

## The perils of democracy

Not everyone was in favor of the idea of democracy. An anonymous political pamphlet from the Age of Pericles summarizes a number of arguments against democracy that were widespread in Athens at the time. Although the pamphleteer argues against these opinions, he nevertheless offers a good impression of the anti-democratic viewpoint.

Against equal participation in government for all citizens, he writes: "One can argue that not everyone should be allowed to speak and sit on the council, but only the best and most intelligent citizens … how can such a low person decide what is good for himself or for the entire populace?" The main objection of the critics of democracy was that effective government was impossible when left to the less educated members of society.

This was certainly the view of the Athenian philosopher Plato (c. 428–348 BCE). In his dialogue *The Republic*, he called democracy anarchy. He wrote: "Whenever a meeting must be held concerning matters of state, the one to stand up and offer advice can be a carpenter, a smith, a shoemaker, a merchant, a shipowner, a rich man, a poor man, of good family, or of no family at all, and no one thinks of telling him that his meddling is not justified by any knowledge of matters, nor by the instruction of a teacher."

There were certainly other citizens in democratic Athens who held such opinions, and who favored an oligarchy (government by the few), even if they played no significant political role. They were admirers of Sparta, a state where, it was said, everyone knew his place. Only in the last quarter of the fifth century BCE, when Athens was at war with Sparta, did the supporters of oligarchy have the opportunity to attempt to change Athenian democracy. Their efforts came to nothing, however.

## The culture of the golden age

During its golden age, Athens was both powerful and prosperous. The city's wealth came from the silver mines of Attica and the harbor dues of Piraeus, which was now the most important port in the eastern Mediterranean region.

The Athenian golden age saw an explosion of creativity in philosophy, art, architecture, and science. For the first time, Athens became an important center for philosophy and science. Philosophers gathered there from all corners of the world, finding a warm welcome among the richer citizens. Among the leading figures who congregated in Athens were Anaxagoras, Socrates, and Plato.

Athens was also visited by sophists— traveling teachers who specialized in teaching intellectual skills, particularly rhetoric and disputation. One of these sophists was Damon, who was also a master of music. He had a special influence on Pericles, as did the Ionian philosopher Anaxagoras. Throughout his life, Pericles was noted for his eloquence, wisdom, and patriotism, which won him recognition from the majority of the citizens of Athens. Although he remained aloof from most Athenians, he had a number of distinguished friends, includ-

*This bronze statue of a Greek warrior dates to the fifth century BCE.*

*This jug, made in Athens in the fifth century BCE, is illustrated with a picture of a woman spinning thread.*

the colony of Thurii on the Gulf of Tarentum in southern Italy. Thurii was intended to be a model colony, taking in emigrants from all over Greece, the Aegean islands, and Ionia and molding them into an ideal community. Many famous figures became involved. The philosopher Protagoras of Abdera is said to have written its laws, while the famous architect and urban designer Hippodamus of Miletus drew up city plans for the colony. Hippodamus had designed Piraeus, which featured a street plan of straight streets crossing each other to flank rectangular blocks of buildings. Because of this connection, some historians believe that Thurii may have had a similar plan, but this has not yet been confirmed by archaeological excavation.

The literary arts flourished in Athens under Pericles. In the theater, Greek tragedy reached its peak, with the plays of Aeschylus, Sophocles, and Euripides being performed. The great comedy writer Aristophanes was also working at this time.

## Architecture

After the destruction of the Acropolis by the Persians in 480 BCE, the Athenians had vowed never to build there again. As they regained confidence and power during the fifth century BCE, this viewpoint gradually changed. To mark the peace with Persia of 449 BCE, Pericles initiated a great building program on the Acropolis, both to restore the temples destroyed by the Persians and to construct new buildings.

The years between 447 and 406 BCE saw the completion of some of the most outstanding examples of Greek architecture. Among the buildings constructed during that period were the Propylaea, the Erechtheum, and the Temple of Athena Nike. The most famous product of this construction program, however, was the Parthenon.

ing the playwright Sophocles, the historian Herodotus, the sculptor Phidias, and the sophist Protagoras. Pericles never married, but he had a mistress, Aspasia. She was a *hetaira*, a sophisticated, highly educated type of prostitute.

One project that had personal interest for Pericles was the development of

# MARRIAGE IN ANCIENT ATHENS

In ancient Athens, marriage was seen as a practical rather than a romantic arrangement; citizens were expected to marry and to procreate. Usually, the fathers of the bride and groom made a contractual agreement for a dowry to be paid by the bride's family to the groom, although the agreement could occasionally be between the groom himself and the bride's father.

The main purpose of a marriage was to produce legitimate children, who would be citizens of Athens. So, an Athenian citizen had to marry another Athenian citizen; otherwise, the children of the marriage would not be deemed citizens. The wedding was celebrated by a wedding feast, held in the house of the bride's family. After the feast, the bridegroom led his veiled wife to his own house, followed by well-wishers who usually sang outside the bridal chamber.

The bride was generally much younger than her bridegroom. In classical Athens, she would typically be around 14, and he might be in his late twenties. Greek society was strictly patriarchal, and the young wife had a subordinate position. Her place was in the home, and in theory, she would leave it only rarely to attend funerals and religious celebrations. In practice, however, there were many religious events in which women played an important role.

In Greek society, women were generally thought to be inferior beings. Men viewed women largely in terms of their bodies—

they were categorized into four groups by their ability to bear children. These groups were the young, sexually immature girl; the marriageable virgin; the sexually active, fertile wife and mother; and the elderly, infertile woman. Outside of this classification, and essentially outside of society, fell unmarried women who had lost their virginity, infertile women, and prostitutes.

A marriage could be ended by divorce. For the husband, this was a simple matter of just banishing his wife from the house. The wife could also leave, but she would probably be unable to obtain the return of her dowry. For this, she would have to go to the courts, which, like so many other things in Greece, were dominated by men and would be unlikely to find in her favor.

*A man is shown leading his bride in this illustration of a wedding scene on a Greek pyxis (jewelry box). In ancient Athens, women married when they were very young.*

A marble temple dedicated to Athena, the Parthenon took its name from one of the goddess's titles, Athena Parthenos, meaning Athena the Virgin. Work began on the building in 447 BCE, yet it was not completed until 438 BCE. The building works were carried out under the direction of the sculptor Phidias. He was also responsible for one of the most imposing features of the temple, a statue of the goddess that stood 40 feet (12 m) high. Made of gold and ivory, it was one of the most admired pieces of art of the ancient world. It is believed to have been destroyed by fire.

The building program provided employment for the city's poorer citizens, while making Athens the most magnificent city of the ancient world. This blossoming of culture, art, and architecture in the fifth century BCE is evidence of the preeminent position Athens held in Greece at that time.

**See also:**

The Birth of Drama (volume 3, page 318) • From Tyranny to Democracy (volume 3, page 294) • The Peloponnesian War (volume 3, page 368) • The Persian Wars (volume 3, page 326)

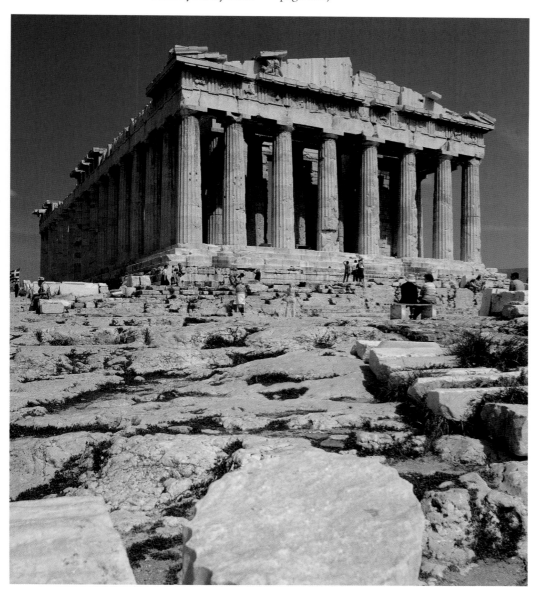

*The Parthenon is the most famous of all the temples built during the Age of Pericles.*

# THE GREAT PHILOSOPHERS

From the sixth century BCE, Greece was home to a number of famous philosophers. Men such as Socrates, Plato, Aristotle, Pythagoras, and Diogenes came up with ideas that were to shape the history of Western thought.

Like most ancient peoples, the Greeks worshipped a variety of gods, who they believed could influence human affairs. However, from the sixth century BCE onward, there was also a general growth of secular thinking. The fifth-century-BCE physician Hippocrates searched for a natural, rather than a supernatural, explanation for disease, while the historian Thucydides made no allowance for the actions of the gods in his account of events of the past. The philosopher Protagoras, also of the fifth century BCE, claimed that there was no absolute "right" and "wrong"—only what human opinion determined was so. This idea was expressed in his famous saying "Man is the measure of all things."

Some thinkers, such as Diagoras of Melos (c. fifth century BCE), went so far as to doubt the existence of the gods. However, even for people who did not possess such extreme views, the relationship between the gods, fate, and man's own responsibility became increasingly a matter for debate in the fifth and fourth centuries BCE, which contributed to the growth of Greek philosophy.

## Ionian philosophy

Greek philosophy had its origins in the sixth century BCE in Ionia. Ionia was a region in western Anatolia that had been occupied by Greeks since around 1000 BCE. People who lived there were more open to influences from other lands and cultures than the citizens of the city-states of mainland Greece. They would have been aware of intellectual accomplishments such as the discoveries of the Babylonian astronomers. These new ideas opened the way for discussions about natural phenomena and gave rise to the birth of philosophy and science.

These new "natural philosophers" tried to describe and explain the origin and existence of heaven and earth in a rational manner, rather than through myths involving the various gods. The philosophers were searching for basic rational principles that could explain the entire universe.

## The School of Miletus

The center of the explosion of new ideas was Miletus, a city on the southwest coast of Ionia. The first of these thinkers (now considered to be the founder of Greek philosophy) was Thales of Miletus, who lived from around 610 to 540 BCE. In the first half of the sixth century BCE, Thales rejected a mytho-

**The School of Athens**, *painted by Raphael in 1510 CE, depicts some of ancient Greece's greatest philosophers, including Plato (center left), Aristotle (center right), and Diogenes (bottom right).*

**Thales of Miletus, shown in this undated modern illustration, is considered to be the father of Greek philosophy.**

the east and possibly also from Egypt in the south. Thales is said to have visited Egypt, where he calculated the height of a pyramid. He subsequently introduced geometry to the Greek world, using Egyptian examples and applications. Because of his practice of making careful observations in order to draw conclusions about the physical nature of the world, Thales has sometimes been called the first scientist. He formulated a theory that the original principle matter of the cosmos was water, from which everything proceeds and into which everything is eventually resolved.

## Anaximander

Anaximander of Miletus (c. 611–546 BCE) was, if anything, even more brilliant than Thales, his teacher, was. Anaximander recorded his theories about the nature of the cosmos in a treatise called *About Nature*. Much of this work is now lost, although the substance of it is referred to by later writers.

According to Anaximander, the entire cosmos was created and derived from something that he called the *apeiron*, which can be translated as "the indeterminate" or "the unlimited." Everything originated from the *apeiron*, which he defined as the first element, and everything would return to it. Anaximander is credited with having produced a sundial and the first Greek map of the world. He is also believed to have introduced a number of hypotheses about astronomy. According to Roman writers of the third century CE, Anaximander also came up with a remarkable theory about the development of life on earth. He believed that humans developed from embryos that were once found inside of fish, a theory that predated the evolutionary theories of Charles Darwin by more than 2,300 years.

Anaximenes of Miletus, a student of Anaximander, was active in the second

logical explanation of the universe and attempted to explain it in rational terms. Thales left no writings of his own, but his beliefs are discussed in Aristotle's *Metaphysics*, a work written in the fourth century BCE. Thales was noted for his knowledge of astronomy. He is reputed to have predicted the solar eclipse of May 28, 585 BCE. To make this calculation, Thales would have used mathematical techniques borrowed from Babylon in half of the sixth century BCE. The last of the three great scholars of the School of Miletus, Anaximenes proposed a system of philosophy based on the idea that a primary element was the origin of all things and beings, including the gods. This primary element was air. Air, he argued, could be transformed into water, earth, and fire. This theory explained the origins of the four elements that were seen as being basic to nature—earth, water, air, and fire. A saying of his sums up his concept: "As the soul, which is breath, holds us together, so does air hold the whole world together."

## Xenophanes

Two other main thinkers who contributed to Ionian natural philosophy were Xenophanes and Heraclitus. Xenophanes was a poet-philosopher who lived from around 580 to 480 BCE. He was born in Colophon, not far from Miletus, but left his place of birth when it came under Persian rule. He settled in the Greek city of Elea in southern Italy, where he is believed to have founded the school of philosophy that was later made famous by Parmenides.

Xenophanes roamed through southern Italy, Sicily, and probably the Greek mainland until old age, reciting his poetry, through which he criticized the opinions of his contemporaries. He was particularly scathing about the accepted mythical explanations of the world and the fact that people believed the gods resembled humans. In attacking how human beings worshipped gods that looked like themselves, he suggested that if cows or horses could draw, they would portray their gods as cows or horses. He also spoke out against wealth, soothsaying, the drinking parties of the nobility, and the idolization of the winners of the Olympic Games. In the last case, he emphasized that it was better to honor a scholar than an athlete because, he said, a

learned man could be of benefit in the managing of the polis, and wise counsel could even bring money. Xenophanes' criticisms were based on his conviction that sensory perceptions were always deceptive and, consequently, could not lead to sure knowledge. Sure knowledge could only reside in the divine—an invisible and omnipresent god.

## Heraclitus

Heraclitus of Ephesus, who probably lived from around 560 to 480 BCE, expressed his ideas in a series of proverbs. His main theory was that the entire cosmos is organized and directed by a single principle, called the Logos in Greek. The material embodiment of this Logos was fire, which Heraclitus considered to be the essential form of matter. The logos is the directing force that ensures equilibrium in the world by balancing change in one area with an equivalent and opposite change elsewhere. One of Heraclitus's best-known sayings, attributed to him by the later philosopher Plato (c. 428–348 BCE), was that "all things are in flux."

*This 15th-century-CE illustration depicts Anaximenes, one of the three great philosophers from the School of Miletus.*

355

## Anaxagoras

One result of the Persian drive into Anatolia in the fifth century BCE was the emigration of Ionian scholars to the Greek mainland and its colonies. Anaxagoras (c. 500–428 BCE), who was born in Clazomenae in Ionia, moved to Athens around 480 BCE. In contrast to earlier thinkers who looked to earth, air, fire, and water for the origin of ultimate reality, Anaxagoras formulated the doctrine of nous (meaning eternal intelligence, from the Greek for "mind" or "reason"). In a work entitled *On Nature*, only portions of which survive, he suggested that all matter existed in a state of chaos as infinitely numerous and small particles called "seeds." These seeds were brought into order by the animating force of nous.

Anaxagoras taught in Athens for 30 years, during which time his students included the dramatist Euripides and possibly also the philosopher Socrates (469–399 BCE). He was also friends with Pericles, but the Athenian statesman was unable to help Anaxagoras when he was charged with impiety for insisting that the stars, including the sun, were glowing masses of red hot stone and that the moon received its light from the sun. For these ideas—far ahead of their time—Anaxagoras was sentenced to death, but he managed to escape to Lampsacus in Anatolia.

## Pythagoras

Thinkers leaving Ionia set up schools of philosophy in southern Italy and Sicily as well as in Athens. One of these thinkers was Pythagoras (c. 580–500 BCE), who was born on the island of Samos off the coast of Anatolia. In his late twenties, apparently unhappy with the policies of the Samian tyrant Polycrates, Pythagoras left Samos for Croton, a Greek colony in southern Italy, where he settled around 530 BCE.

In Croton, Pythagoras established a philosophical sect that had two main

*In ancient Greece, solar eclipses were mysterious events. Thales of Miletus is believed to be the first person to predict one successfully.*

*Helios the sun god rides across the sky in his chariot in this vase painting. The philosopher Xenophanes ridiculed people who believed that the gods looked like humans.*

teachings. One idea was that the study of mathematics and numbers could reveal the hidden order of the universe. The other idea was the doctrine of metempsychosis, which stated that at death the soul passes into another body, either that of a human or that of an animal.

The fact that the Pythagorean movement was a sect was important. It was the first time in the history of Greek religion that a group had distinguished itself in this way. At first, the Pythagoreans had great influence in Croton, but the residents of the city came to distrust the sect so much that around 500 BCE they set fire to the Pythagorean building. The embittered Pythagoras left the city for another Greek colony close by called Metapontion, where he died within a short time.

An important part of Pythagoras's teaching was the concept of purity and *ascesis* (training or exercise). He asserted that anyone who does not succeed in keeping his body pure by following the rules of life also contaminates his soul.

Unjust behavior also pollutes the soul, which is then not capable of achieving *sophia* (wisdom or insight).

According to Pythagoras's followers, someone's conduct in life could affect his or her eternal fate. An immoral life could lead to reincarnation as an animal. Pythagoreans believed that the main goal in life is to attain as much *sophia* as possible, so the soul rises toward a better body in the next life.

## Music and mathematics

After Pythagoras's death, his disciples continued to develop his ideas. In mathematics, they searched for patterns, believing that the essence of all things lay in numbers and that all relationships could be expressed numerically. Music, in particular, could be explained by mathematical formulas. Pythagoras's followers discovered that if a string of a stringed instrument is stopped halfway along its length, it will produce a note one octave higher than the note of the whole string.

*Anaxagoras, shown in this 15th-century-CE illustration, was one of the first astronomers to believe that the moon received its light from the sun.*

whom was Parmenides of Elea. Elea was a small Greek colony on the southwest coast of Italy, and it was there that Parmenides was born in 515 BCE. Growing up in a wealthy and powerful family, he became a politician before founding a school of philosophy in his home town.

## An ideal world

The heart of the philosophy of Parmenides was that the material world is unreal; reality only subsists in a timeless "ideal world," an idea that may have owed something to the Pythagoreans. Parmenides expressed his ideas in a poem, large parts of which have survived. He believed that all movement is nothing other than outward appearance. Only "being" exists; there is no "not being." The "being" is like a sphere—perfect and indivisible.

The radical nature of Parmenides' philosophy is evident when compared to that of the great Ionian philosophers of the seventh and sixth centuries BCE. They supposed that all things were derived from a basic element—whether water, fire, air, or earth—and assumed that the contraction of that element brought about changes in nature. When an element assumes a material form, however, it must necessarily occupy a place that was originally empty—a vacuum. This vacuum is what Parmenides called "not being." Because he believed that such a vacuum could not exist, he considered the entire philosophy of the Ionian school invalid.

In geometry, the Pythagoreans established the famous theorem that the square of the hypotenuse (the longest side) of a right-angled triangle is equal to the sum of the squares of the other two sides. This theorem is still taught in schools today.

The Pythagoreans were among the first to teach that the Earth is a spherical planet that revolves around a fixed point. They also saw a numerical scheme behind the arrangement of the heavenly bodies. Pythagoras's followers believed that these bodies were separated from each other by intervals corresponding to the harmonic length of strings. The very movement of the heavenly bodies, they contended, produced music—the "harmony of the spheres."

The teachings of Pythagoras had a considerable influence on many Greek thinkers of the fifth century BCE, one of

*Pythagoras, shown in this 17th-century-CE illustration, is identified with the theorem about the lengths of the sides of a right-angled triangle.*

In this 15th-century-CE woodcut, Pythagoras demonstrates the relationship between music and mathematics.

## ACHILLES AND THE TURTLE

One of Zeno's famous paradoxes is the story of Achilles and the turtle. Achilles, the fastest runner among the Greeks, challenges a turtle, the slowest of animals, to a race. Achilles gives the turtle a head start of a certain distance, and then they start to run at the same time. When Achilles comes to the place where the turtle started, the turtle has run a certain distance and is ahead of Achilles. Achilles keeps running, but every time he arrives at the place where the turtle was, the turtle has also run a certain distance farther. As fast as Achilles runs, and as slow as the turtle crawls, there will always be a distance for Achilles yet to cover. In other words, Achilles can never catch up with the turtle. This paradox rests on the assumption of infinite divisibility. On the basis of such clever absurdities, which appealed enormously to the Greeks, Zeno attempted to demonstrate the truth of the "indivisibility of being"—and thus that Parmenides was right.

Parmenides also believed it was impossible to explain motion in a philosophical manner. When an object moves from one place to another, he believed, something must be moved that was there before, or the object has to move to a place where there was nothing. Even when the object is initially moved to a place where it replaces another object, there must come a time when the moved object comes to a stop on a place where there was nothing—a vacuum. A vacuum (a "not being") cannot exist, so consequently, neither can motion, from Parmenides' viewpoint.

Zeno (c. 495–430 BCE), a student of Parmenides, tried to prove his teacher's theory of the "indivisibility of being" by means of a number of paradoxes, the most famous of which is that of Achilles and the turtle. In spite of all their logic, these stories led their readers to conclusions that seemed totally absurd. For this reason, the stories exercised the minds of Greek thinkers for lengthy periods of time.

## Atomic theory

Another of Parmenides' students was Leucippus (c. fifth century BCE), the founder of the theory of atoms. In Greek, the word *atomos* means "something that is not divisible." Leucippus argued that all matter consists of countless tiny particles, or atoms, and that the diversity of matter depends on the way in which these atoms are combined. The point over which Leucippus stumbled was that he had to allow for empty space, or a vacuum, between the atoms, which brought him into conflict with the ideas of his master.

The work commenced by Leucippus was continued by his student Democritus of Abdera, who perfected the theory of atoms. Democritus maintained that visible reality is made up of atoms, which are in eternal motion in endless space. Atoms are unchangeable but infinitely varied, and by joining together, they form all living and non-living matter.

Greek thinkers of the sixth and fifth centuries BCE were obsessed with questions that were actually unsolvable by philosophers. However, while seeking answers to these questions, some of the philosophers discovered mathematical and scientific truths that were way ahead of their time.

## The sophists

In spite of their importance in the development of Western thought, the early philosophers did not have the same social influence as the fifth-century sophists. The sophists were teachers who traveled from city to city, offering to tutor young

*An artist's impression of the inside of an atom. The Greek philosopher Leucippus was responsible for one of the world's earliest atomic theories.*

men in intellectual skills such as public speaking. The Greek word *sophistes* originally meant "expert" or "man of wisdom," but it gradually acquired a different connotation.

The negative image of the sophists arose because they excelled at rhetoric and taught would-be public speakers how to look at a question from both sides and defend both viewpoints. Consequently, a sophist came to be regarded as someone who was very clever with words and could convince an unsuspecting listener of just about anything. Good or bad, the sophist could make a good argument for it.

Initially, the sophists were quite popular in Athens, but they eventually drew fire from Socrates, Plato, and Aristotle, as well as the state itself, for their indifference to morality. Plato and Aristotle also criticized the sophists for taking money, even though, as itinerant educators, that was how they earned their living.

The term *sophist* came to acquire a derogatory meaning, and the word *sophistry* was defined as "deceptive or false reasoning." On one occasion, Socrates compared the sophist to a fisherman: Both try to fish—one to catch his meal, the other to catch people to cheat them out of their money in exchange for false teachings.

## Socrates

The philosopher Socrates was of seminal importance to the development of Western thought. Unlike most Greek philosophers, he came from humble origins, being the son of Sophroniscus, a sculptor, and Phaenarete, a midwife. It is

*Socrates, shown in this 20th-century-CE illustration, is considered to be one of the greatest philosophers of all time. His teachings survive through the work of his pupil Plato.*

From a relatively early age, Socrates wanted to be a philosopher and to guide the moral and intellectual improvement of Athens. In order to do so, he turned an otherwise normal life into one of public dialogue in the marketplaces and squares of Athens. However, Socrates wrote no books and established no formal school of philosophy. What is known about him and his thinking comes primarily from the works of his student Plato and, to a lesser extent, from the historian Xenophon. It is through the writings of these two men that Socrates has been able to exert his profound influence on all later Western thinking.

## A matter of ethics

Socrates rejected the conflicting ideas of the "one," the "indivisible," and the "eternally changeable." He also refused to become involved in the search for the "core of things" or "basic matter." His interest was in ethics and in the objective definition of love, justice, and virtue, achieved through rational argument. He argued that all vice is the result of ignorance and that no one is intentionally wicked. Because those who know what is right will act rightly, virtue is the result of knowledge.

Sophocles despised rhetoric and long-winded arguments about nothing. Consequently, he ridiculed the sophists and rhetoricians. He was relentless in employing logic as a weapon in his philosophical duels. In these "battles," clarity and simplicity had the highest priority, and in his arguments, he used expressions and terms derived from daily life. Plato recorded how Socrates managed to embarrass Gorgias, one of the most famous sophists of Athens, simply by plying him with question after question.

Plato also recorded an encounter between Socrates and the two great philosophers of Elea, Parmenides and Zeno. The two Elean philosophers had

not known who his teachers were, but he seems to have been acquainted with the doctrines of Parmenides, Heraclitus, and Anaxagoras. However, far from pursuing their ideas, he was more interested in ethical matters, such as how a man should conduct himself in life.

There is no clear indication as to how Socrates supported himself. He apparently worked as a sculptor for a while; his statue of the Three Graces stood near the entrance to the Acropolis until the second century CE. It is also known that he fought as a hoplite for Athens in the Peloponnesian War, serving with distinction in the campaign of Potidaea in 432–430 BCE.

traveled to Athens to attend the Panathenaea and were staying at the home of Plato's stepbrother. One morning, Socrates visited the famous guests and subjected them to his relentless questioning. Parmenides kindly attempted to answer Socrates' questions, while Zeno did his best to get the troublesome visitor out of the door.

Socrates then summed up his impressions of the two philosophers: "I understand that Zeno is actually a second Parmenides, even though he says things in a totally different manner. You, Parmenides, want to convince us that everything is one, and Zeno says, on the other hand, that diversity cannot exist. So you argue in two different manners to express the same truth: one of you claims something, and the other repudiates the opposite. Something like this demands a mental effort that far exceeds my moderate abilities."

Socrates' attitude toward the two philosophers from Elea illustrates his manner of disputation. He typically presented himself as someone who needed things explained to him. This profession of ignorance, given his brilliance and extraordinary sharpness of mind, is called Socratic irony. By constantly questioning his interlocutor and forcing him to define his terms, Socrates' aim was to encourage people to think for themselves and seek eternal truths.

## The pursuit of knowledge

Socrates started from the basic principle that only the good can guide the behavior of man, and man must strive toward knowing that good. When man has found that out, he will pursue it—no one will ever go deliberately against the good. Socrates' philosophical enquiries took the form of a conversation or dialogue—starting from the specific, he

**The Death of Socrates** *was painted by Jacques-Louis David in 1787 CE. Socrates was condemned to death for heresy and died by taking hemlock.*

sought general truths through an endless game of question and answer. Even though his method was based on logic and rationality, Socrates also accepted that there was something like "the voice of one's own conscience"—an instinctive, nonrational sense of higher values that could keep a man from committing wrongful actions.

Unlike the sophists, Socrates refused to gather paying students around him. Instead, he would present questions to anyone who talked to him at any time. He elicited answers that, after subjecting them to acute analysis mixed with mild derision, he rejected as inadequate or incorrect. He then attempted to reach a logical and correct conclusion, encouraging his "victim" to formulate clear-cut definitions. This goal was hardly ever achieved, but the value of the discussion lay in the enlightenment of both people involved.

By the end of the fifth century BCE, Socrates had made a lot of enemies in Athens. His criticism of the sophists and of the institution of democracy did not endear him to the general public. In the drama *The Clouds*, Aristophanes made fun of him as the director of a "thinking shop." Eventually, Socrates' enemies managed to get their revenge. In 399 BCE, he was charged with religious heresies and corrupting the morals of Athenian youths.

## The trial of Socrates

In accordance with Athenian law, the accused had to defend himself by means of a public speech. Plato's *Apology* gives an account of Socrates' defending arguments, which exhibited both his ironic style and his simple dialectic. Socrates disputed the Athenian judges' authority to sentence him to death, as his accusers wished, and pointed out great gaps in the official accusation. However, he had clearly determined that if the jury took offense at his life and work, then they had to condemn him. He refused to deny what he had asserted for so many years.

It is possible that Socrates could have avoided his heavy sentence by using a different defense, based less deeply on principle. Had he done so, he might have got off with a fine; there were plenty of

*Plato, originally a pupil of the great philosopher Socrates, eventually became an important figure in his own right.*

his students who would have been happy to pay it for him. Instead, he was sentenced to death, although at first only by a small majority. As allowed by Athenian law, Socrates replied to the sentence—with an ironic proposition that it should be changed to a small fine because his importance to the state was also small. Enraged by his stance, the jury voted again. The result was an increased majority for the death penalty.

Socrates could easily have fled the city; his friends even planned his escape. However, he preferred to comply with the verdict. Plato's *Phaedo* describes the final day of Socrates' life. In the evening, in accordance with the usual method of execution, he drank a fatal cup of the poisonous herb hemlock.

## Plato's Academy

Socrates' student Plato (c. 428–348 BCE) went on to become a distinguished philosopher in his own right. He came from a noble, wealthy family and grew up during the time of the Peloponnesian War. Plato contemplated a political career when he was young, but he became disillusioned with politics, and it was then that he became a follower of Socrates. Plato was greatly influenced by Socrates' method of question and answer in the pursuit of truth.

In 387 BCE, Plato founded his Academy, a school devoted to the pursuit of philosophical knowledge, and it was there that he refined his own philosophical ideas. He considered that only "the idea" was real and rejected the view that

*In this 19th-century-CE illustration, Alexander the Great visits the philosopher Diogenes in his tub. As part of his austere lifestyle, Diogenes lived in a tub in the streets of Athens.*

# THE CYNICS

Some students of Socrates attempted to carry on the work of their master, in particular by practicing asceticism (giving up material pleasures). One of those students was Antisthenes, who founded the movement that was later known as the Cynics. Antisthenes had been a sophist until he came under the influence of Socrates, after which he started to protest against the material interests of established society. He contended that any form of luxury or pleasure made people slaves, and therefore unhappy. Instead, people should free themselves from all needs and strive toward the good; only that approach could offer a happy life.

These ideas were carried to the extreme by Diogenes (c. 400–325 BCE), who was born in Sinope on the coast of the Black Sea. In middle age, he went to Athens, where he became a student of Antisthenes. Diogenes rejected all social conventions and completely embraced poverty and austerity. Homeless and sleeping outdoors, he traveled from city to city expounding his belief in the simple life to all who would listen. His brutish lifestyle earned him the abusive name of *kuon* ("dog"), and from this, his followers came to be called *kunikoi*, or Cynics. Diogenes welcomed the nickname, arguing that if humans lived like dogs, they would be far happier.

*Diogenes was famous for his austere lifestyle. He believed that human society was hypocritical and that it was better to live like a dog with no material possessions. This engraving is based on a 17th-century-CE drawing by Joachim von Sandrart.*

knowledge was based on sensory experience. The object of knowledge (the idea) had to be something fixed, permanent, and unchangeable—it was based on reason, not sensory perception. This approach countered the ideas of most previous philosophers, who had sought to explain reality in terms of the material world. Plato maintained that reality did not reside in the material world but in another world of eternal phenomena that he called Forms. All objects in the material world are merely representations of the eternal Forms.

Applying his theory of knowledge to social philosophy, Plato wrote the *Republic* and the *Laws*. These described an ideal city-state, which could serve as a blueprint for a state on earth. In this state, the philosopher-rulers would exercise control over the two lower classes—peasant-artisans and soldiers. Because the leaders would have true knowledge, there would be no room for dissent. In 367 BCE, Plato tried to persuade the tyrant Dionysius II of Syracuse to put his ideas into practice but did not succeed.

## Aristotle

Aristotle (384–322 BCE) was Plato's most important student. He spent 20 years at Plato's Academy, but while he was strongly influenced by Plato's ideas, his own philosophy developed in a different direction. Aristotle preferred an experimental and deductive approach based on the reasoning of the mind, insisting that the observation of visible reality was of prime importance. His major contribution to philosophy was to establish a system of logic that was to influence philosophical reasoning for more than two thousand years.

In 335 BCE, Aristotle established his own school in Athens, called the Lyceum, where scientific subjects such as biology and physics were studied in addition to philosophy and logic. Aristotle taught at the school but also had time to pursue his own research. He wrote major works on zoology, geography, history, mathematics, and astronomy, which were to be highly influential in medieval times. He also drew up an inventory of all political systems of the time and described an ideal polis that would combine the best elements of existing systems.

**See also:**

The Age of Pericles (volume 3, page 340) •
The Greek Legacy (volume 3, page 404) •
Greek Religion (volume 3, page 310)

*This bust depicts the Greek philosopher Aristotle, a former pupil of Plato.*

# THE PELOPONNESIAN WAR

The Peloponnesian War was a mammoth struggle between Sparta and Athens that took place toward the end of the fifth century BCE. The war lasted for 27 years, from 431 to 404 BCE, and tore the Greek world apart.

The roots of the conflict between Athens and Sparta lay in their cultural differences. By the middle of the fifth century BCE, Athens had become the undisputed artistic and intellectual center of Greece. It was an "open" society, engaging in many commercial transactions with the outside world and depending on large-scale imports of food to feed its population. Athens was a progressive and democratic state, and an expansive naval power. Sparta, on the other hand, was an isolated, agrarian, and largely self-sufficient closed society with an oligarchic government (one dominated by a small elite). While the militaristic Sparta experienced only stagnation, Athens became increasingly self-confident and more aggressive in its foreign affairs.

## Alliances

Both Athens and Sparta had many allies. Athens was backed by the member states of the Delian League, an alliance that had been set up in 477 BCE to protect the Greek cities of Ionia (an area of southwestern Anatolia) and the nearby islands against possible Persian attack. As the Greeks defeated the Persians in successive battles, Athens, with its powerful navy, gradually came to dominate the league, which soon became more of an Athenian empire than a voluntary confederation of independent city-states. On Sparta's side was the Peloponnesian League, a group of city-states located in the Peloponnese (the southern part of mainland Greece).

In the middle of the fifth century BCE, there were occasional skirmishes between Athens and Sparta. The skirmishes ended in 446 BCE, when the two parties signed a peace agreement. The pact was supposed to hold for three decades. In fact, the Thirty Years' Peace lasted only until 431 BCE, when full-scale war broke out.

## The origins of the war

The immediate cause of the war was the fact that Athens assisted the island of Corcyra (present-day Corfu) in its conflict with Corinth, an ally of Sparta. Corcyra had long been a colony of Corinth and, in turn, had founded its own colony, called Epidamnus, on the Adriatic coast of what is now Albania. When a dispute erupted between Epidamnus and Corcyra, Epidamnus called on Corinth for help. Corcyra, feeling threatened by Corinth, decided to join the powerful Delian League. Athens was happy to welcome the island into the coalition, particularly because the addi-

*This vase painting depicts a Greek hoplite of the fifth century BCE. He is armed with the long spear that was typical of the period.*

tion of Corcyra's fleet of 120 war vessels to its own fleet would greatly strengthen the naval power of Athens. A joint force of Athenian and Corcyrean ships clashed with the Corinthian fleet in 433 BCE. The following year, Athens laid siege to Potidaea, a Corinthian colony. Incensed, the Corinthians demanded that Sparta should declare war on Athens.

Archidamus II, king of Sparta, made a final attempt to avoid a confrontation with Athens. As commander-in-chief of the Peloponnesian League, he urged its members to review the situation before acting precipitously. His urging was in vain, however. In 432 BCE, the League voted for war. The following year, Athens in turn declared war on Sparta.

The leading Athenian statesman, Pericles, was confident that Athens was the stronger power. Money collected from the Delian League meant that any campaign would not be short of finance, while the Long Walls gave the Athenians a secure route to the vital port of Piraeus, where there lay a fleet of 200 warships.

Pericles made the decision not to defend Attica on land; his plan was to defeat Sparta at sea. In 431 BCE, the Spartans invaded unopposed, destroying the harvest, cutting down olive trees and grapevines, and demolishing buildings. The raid lasted perhaps a month—historically campaigning seasons were short because soldiers had to return home to tend to their farms. However, the raids became an annual occurrence over the following five years. Pericles retaliated with attacks on Megara and Epidaurus.

## Plague

In 430 BCE, a deadly epidemic broke out in Athens, which was overcrowded with refugees from Attica. The historian

*The island of Corfu, shown here, was known as Corcyra in ancient Greece. A dispute between Corcyra and the city-state of Corinth was the catalyst for the Peloponnesian War.*

*This vase painting depicts a Greek warship. Naval power was a major factor in the Peloponnesian War.*

Thucydides provided a very graphic account of the illness (see box, page 372), which killed around 50,000 people. The psychological effects of this sudden mass death were as serious as the physical consequences of the epidemic. Believing they might be struck down and die within days, people began to live for the moment, squandering their wealth and committing many acts without regard for the law. According to Thucydides, "they did not believe they would live long enough to be prosecuted and punished by the judiciary."

## A change of leadership

When Pericles fell victim to the epidemic in 429 BCE, the leadership of Athens fell to Cleon, the major representative of the pro-war party. Together with the general Demosthenes, Cleon spearheaded several victories, notably the crushing of Spartan forces at the Battle of Pylos in 425 BCE. However, in 422 BCE, Cleon's luck changed abruptly. In a battle to recapture the Athenian colony of Amphipolis, which had fallen to the

## THE LONG WALLS

Some 30 years before the outbreak of the Peloponnesian War, the Athenian statesman Pericles initiated the building of two walls to safeguard the route between Athens and its port Piraeus. Between 461 and 456 BCE, two great walls were constructed, enclosing a roadway around 600 feet (183 m) wide. The Long Walls turned the whole Athens-Piraeus complex into a single fortress, ensuring that Athens had unrestricted access to the fleet at Piraeus. When Attica was invaded by the Spartans during the Peloponnesian War, its citizens took refuge in Athens, and many were crammed between the Long Walls. The difficult and unsanitary conditions greatly contributed to the catastrophic outbreak of the plague in 430 BCE.

## THUCYDIDES' ACCOUNT OF THE PLAGUE

When the plague broke out in Athens in 430 BCE, the historian Thucydides was living in the city. He wrote extensively about the plague, noting that it claimed more victims than all of Sparta's campaigns combined. He went on: "I want to discuss this illness so that able physicians may determine whence this evil came and which causes may have produced such a calamity. If this illness returns, everyone shall be warned and take measures. I speak of this epidemic as someone who knows it intimately, for I too was affected and I saw many fall ill and die.

"That year had been extraordinarily healthy and free of all other disease. But if someone sustained a wound or became ill, it immediately turned into this pestilence. The healthy were suddenly afflicted, without there being any evident reason for their illness. First they felt a severe headache; their eyes turned red, their throat became inflamed and their breathing became labored. Hoarseness, pain in the chest, and a mucous cough were followed by painful contractions and convulsions, which lasted longer with some than with others. The skin swelled up and turned red and became covered with small blisters of pus. Some died after seven or nine days as a result of a burning pain in their intestines. Those still living after this time were struck with stomach pains. After severe diarrhea and cramps, most succumbed from total exhaustion.

"Generally, the contagion appeared first on the head and subsequently spread over the entire body. Some were blinded or paralyzed; others went mad and did not recognize friends or relatives. Although there were many unburied corpses lying out in the open, the vultures and other scavengers did not come near them, and when they did eat the diseased human flesh, they also died."

*Still a bustling commercial center today, Piraeus has been the port of Athens since ancient times. During the Peloponnesian War, Athens and the port were connected by fortified walls.*

Spartan general Brasidas, Cleon was killed. Brasidas also died.

With the leading proponent for war on either side dead, the stage was clear for peace negotiations. On Cleon's death, the Athenian general Nicias became the leading Athenian politician, and he negotiated a peace agreement with Sparta and the Peloponnesian League. The Peace of Nicias was intended to last for 50 years. In fact, it broke down in less than three.

## Alcibiades

Alcibiades (c. 450–404 BCE) was a young, ambitious nobleman who, having lost his father at an early age, had been reared by his uncle, Pericles. Spoiled but handsome, Alcibiades used his charm to secure great personal popularity. Contemporary sources describe his great appetite for power as well as his sexual and other excesses.

In 420 BCE, when he was around 30 years old, Alcibiades was called on by the Athenian people to act as one of the ten *strategoi* (chief military commanders). It was not a good decision. Alcibiades was keen to win honors on the battlefield, even though the Peace of Nicias had only just been negotiated. Alcibiades was a staunch political opponent of the

treaty, and he sought to stir up some trouble for Sparta by playing on the dissatisfaction that some members of the Peloponnesian League felt with the conditions set forth in the recent peace agreement. He persuaded Athens to join with the disaffected cities of Argos, Mantinea, and Elis in confronting Sparta at the Battle of Mantinea in 418 BCE. The result was a resounding victory for the Spartans.

Undaunted by this setback, Alcibiades sought to revive the policies of Pericles, who had aspired to found an empire in the west with Thurii, in southern Italy, as its center. The Athenian fleet already controlled the Aegean Sea, the Dardanelles, and the Bosporus, so Alcibiades argued that if Athens could extend its dominion to the western basin of the Mediterranean, Sparta would be completely isolated on the Peloponnese.

### Sicilian campaign

The primary objective of Alcibiades' plan was to gain control of Sicily, which he considered a bridgehead to both southern Italy and Africa. A large number of Athenians enthusiastically supported this scheme, but several cautious men, including Nicias and Socrates, opposed the enterprise. A decision in favor of war was made after a delegation from Sicily visited Athens. The party consisted of representatives of several Sicilian cities, who claimed that they felt threatened by the powerful Dorian city of Syracuse, an ally of Sparta, that dominated

*This statue depicts the Athenian nobleman Alcibiades, who defected to Sparta when he was accused of sacrilege.*

the island. Alcibiades' plan encountered little further resistance from the Athenian assembly. Nicias, Lamachus, and Alcibiades were appointed leaders of a military expedition to Sicily to capture Syracuse. A fleet of around 260 ships was fitted out. On board were more than 5,000 heavily armed hoplites, in addition to thousands of support troops.

## Disaster in Sicily

From the moment the fleet reached Sicily in 415 BCE, everything went wrong. The island's Greek colonies were not willing to participate in the campaign against Syracuse. Nor did they want to bear the heavy cost of provisioning the Athenian troops, which forced the expedition's leaders to look outside the city walls, where makeshift markets sold supplies at monstrously inflated prices. The cities of Tarentum and Locris even refused to supply fresh water.

In spite of such setbacks, the Athenians succeeded in taking the city of Catana, which was strategically important because it lay between Syracuse and Messina and could be used to command the strait between Sicily and southern Italy. The aim was to isolate Syracuse and enable the Athenians to find allies among the discontented cities on the other side of the strait.

By this point, Alcibiades was no longer involved in the campaign, however, because he had been recalled to

*The Temple to Apollo in Syracuse. The Athenians unsuccessfully tried to capture the city in the Peloponnesian War.*

Athens on a charge of sacrilege. The accusation was that he had "mocked the goddesses of Eleusis and ridiculed their mysteries." On the return voyage to Athens, he escaped his captors and fled to Sparta, where he became a counselor to the enemies of his native city.

## Syracuse

In the spring of 414 BCE, the aging Nicias took command of the Athenian troops on Sicily and started a siege of Syracuse. The Athenians attempted to isolate the city by building a siege wall on land while their fleet kept the Syracuse warships confined to the harbor. However, the arrival of a Spartan general, Gylippus, with a Peloponnesian force put an end to Athenian hopes of a swift victory. Suddenly, the Athenians were on the defensive. Nicias was forced to send a desperate message to Athens for more troops. Athens responded with a second army and support fleet, but neither was able to salvage the expedition.

When, in September of 413 BCE, Nicias finally decided to abandon the siege of Syracuse, the retreat degenerated into a debacle. The Athenian troops were surrounded and either massacred or taken prisoner. The commanders, including Nicias, were summarily executed. The other prisoners either became forced laborers in the mines of Syracuse, where they died slow deaths, or were sold into slavery.

The Sicilian campaign was a disaster for Athens. The campaign had been immensely expensive, and the whole expeditionary force of both

*This Greek sculpture from the sixth century BCE depicts a hoplite. Hoplites still formed the backbone of Greek armies 200 years later.*

men and warships was wiped out. The Athenian spirit was undaunted, however. The war on the Greek mainland, in the Aegean, and in Ionia was to continue for another nine years.

## The end of Alcibiades

Alcibiades established a niche for himself in Sparta as a strategic advisor on the Syracuse campaign. However, his position there became much less secure once the Athenian expeditionary force was destroyed. He fled to Anatolia and settled in the court of the Persian governor, where he tried to persuade the Persians to conclude an alliance with Athens against Sparta. This plan failed, driving the distrustful Persians into the arms of Sparta instead. In 411 BCE, following some political unrest in Athens, Alcibiades was reinstated as an Athenian army commander and won some victories for Athens in the Aegean. Toward the end of the war, however, he lost the trust of the Athenian people for a second time. He once again fled to the Persians, who killed him.

## The defeat of Athens

After the disastrous Sicilian campaign, the war continued, being mainly fought in the Aegean and Ionia. Because so many Athenian ships had been destroyed at Syracuse, Sparta's sea power now more than equaled that of Athens. To make matters worse for Athens, Persia lent financial support to Sparta and helped it to build a new fleet. In 404 BCE, the beleaguered

# THUCYDIDES

Much of what is known about the Peloponnesian War is derived from the work of the historian Thucydides (c. 460–400 BCE). Born into a wealthy Athenian family, Thucydides lived through the war, and from its beginning, he set out to document it as objectively as possible. Unlike his predecessor Herodotus, Thucydides recorded events in chronological order without reference to the work of fate or the meddling of the gods.

Thucydides took the view that events were the result of both the circumstances of the time and the characters of the leading personalities involved. He had the advantage of firsthand knowledge of many of the events, and indeed took part in the war himself at one point. In 424 BCE, he was elected as a *strategos*, given the command of the Athenian fleet, and ordered to go to the assistance of Amphipolis, which was under siege by the Spartans. However, he arrived too late to save the city from being taken, and for this blunder, he was banished from Athens. He spent the next 20 years in exile, but he used the time to travel extensively around the Greek region, gathering material for his great *History of the Peloponnesian War*.

Thucydides visited Sparta, which he compared unfavorably with Athens in the following words: "If the city of Sparta were to be depopulated so that only the temples and public buildings remained, then I believe that in due course someone visiting the city would not be able to believe that Sparta had been as powerful a state as it currently is. But if the city of Athens were to have the same fate, a person visiting it later would think that it had been even greater and more powerful than it actually is today—just from seeing the ruins and the enormous space they occupy."

Thucydides' comparison was prophetic. Anyone traveling to Sparta today will find an insignificant rural town without many monuments. Athens, on the other hand, still boasts numerous ruins of temples, theaters, marketplaces, and other great monuments, despite its eventful and sometimes violent history.

*This bust depicts the Greek historian Thucydides. His* History of the Peloponnesian War *is the main source of knowledge about the military struggles between Athens and Sparta in the fifth century BCE.*

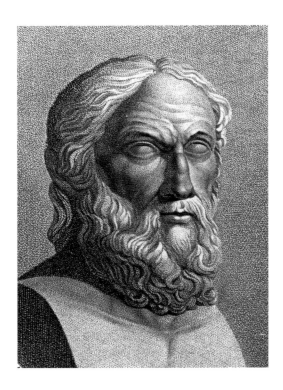

*This 19th-century-CE engraving depicts the playwright Aristophanes. Many of his works ridiculed warlike politicians.*

and isolated Athens was forced to surrender. The Delian League was dissolved, the Athenian fleet was destroyed, and the walls of Athens were razed.

## The aftermath of the war

At the end of the war, Athens was occupied by the Spartan general Lysander, who proposed that in place of the former democracy, the city should be ruled by an oligarchy. Thirty Athenians were appointed to govern the city. With Lysander's approval, they proceeded to seize absolute power. Backed by Spartan troops, the Thirty Tyrants immediately set about settling accounts with their former political opponents. All democratic institutions were abolished, and with the help of their own police force, the tyrants confiscated property, arrested

## ARISTOPHANES AND THE WAR

The atmosphere of war appears to have no detrimental effect on the art of theater in Athens. With the city under siege, Attica in flames, and the Athenian fleet threatened with destruction, dramatists such as Euripides and Aristophanes (c. 450–388 BCE) continued to produce tragedies and comedies.

Aristophanes' plays enjoyed great popularity. They were biting satirical comedies in which he mocked both politicians and society. As a comedy writer, his goals were to entertain his audience and to win the annual prize at the festival of Dionysus. His plays about the war describe the atmosphere of the time—firewood is scarce and olive oil expensive, while traitors, defectors, defeatists, and war profiteers abound.

In *Acharnians* (425 BCE), Aristophanes mocks the war and makes a plea for peace, portraying a peasant concluding his own peace with the

Spartans. In *Knights* (424 BCE), he attacks Cleon, the radical democrat, who is portrayed as a scheming slave outwitted by a sausage seller. The warlike Cleon was a frequent target of ridicule in Aristophanes' plays. *Clouds* (423 BCE) is an attack on the sophists and Socrates, while *Wasps* (422 BCE) satirizes the Athenian love of litigation. *Peace* (produced shortly before the Peace of Nicias was signed in 421 BCE) sees a farmer flying to heaven to find the goddess of the title, while the farcical *Lysistrata* (413 BCE) depicts the women of Athens going on sex strike, declaring they will withhold their favors from their husbands until the men end the war and make peace.

In all, 11 of Aristophanes' plays have survived. It is clear from their content that he enjoyed great freedom of speech to mock whatever he disliked in Athenian society and politics, even in a time of war.

*This 19th-century-CE colored lithograph shows the Spartan general Lysander outside the walls of Athens.*

citizens on flimsy charges, and carried out summary executions.

The rule of the Thirty Tyrants was so unbearable that, after only one year, the Athenians rebelled. Opponents of the regime who had fled the city gathered under the exiled Athenian soldier Thrasybulus, and this makeshift army met the forces of the Tyrants and defeat-ed them. The triumphant Athenians then entered the city and executed most of the remaining Thirty, after which, democracy was restored. Surprisingly, Sparta did nothing to stop this turn of events. It seems that the Spartan king, Pausanias, disagreed with Lysander's ruthless treatment of the Athenians and, rather than send out an army to reverse logographers are counted among Attica's best-known orators, even though they never spoke during Athenian legal sessions; not being citizens of Athens, they were not allowed to do so. One of the most famous litigators of the late fifth century BCE was Lysias (c. 459–380 BCE), who was a *metic*, or foreigner residing in Athens.

Lysias was a native of Syracuse. His father acquired such fame as a manufacturer of armor and shields that Pericles invited him to settle in Athens. After their father's death, Lysias and his elder brother moved to Thurii, the Athenian colony in southern Italy, where Lysias learned the art of rhetoric and eloquence from a distinguished orator. After the failure of the Athenian campaign in Sicily, the brothers returned to Athens, where they earned a fortune from the sale of weapons before the end of the Peloponnesian War.

Following the defeat of Athens and the installation of the Thirty Tyrants, the new government instituted a ruthless purge of anyone suspected of democratic sympathies. Scores of people were sent into exile or condemned to death. Lysias's brother was executed, but Lysias himself managed to escape from the city and join the conspirators who were planning to restore democracy. After the Thirty Tyrants were defeated, Lysias returned to Athens. In a major trial, he prosecuted Eratosthenes, one of the Thirty who had survived, for the murder of his brother. Due to the trial's political background, it attracted a large audience.

In his speech, Lysias outlined the crimes that Eratosthenes had committed, together with his role in the Thirty Tyrants' reign of terror. Lysias's words touched on matters that were fresh in the memory of everyone. His indictment of the oligarchs' crimes aided the recovery process that saw democracy reestablish itself in Athens.

*This 18th-century-CE drawing of an ancient Greek bust depicts the Athenian orator Lysias. He was an adversary of the Thirty Tyrants, who ruled Athens after the end of the Peloponnesian War.*

the situation, preferred to recognize the new government.

## The orators

After democracy was restored in Athens in 403 BCE, the city saw a period in which great orators became highly influential in meetings of the public assembly. These orators were for the most part legal experts who were accustomed to arguing a case in the law courts. Because, in theory, anyone accused of a crime in Athens had to argue his own defense, many orators made money by writing speeches for their clients to read in court.

Orators who wrote speeches for other public speakers were known as logographers or storywriters. Several

## Spartan imperialism

Although Athens had won back its freedom, Sparta remained the overlord of all Greece, which had some catastrophic consequences. Sparta's victory in the Peloponnesian War had been achieved with the help of Persian financial aid, and in return, the Ionian Greek cities in Anatolia had to cede their autonomy to Persia once more. Sparta made other cities protectorates and forced them to pay large sums of money in tribute. In effect, this meant that Athenian imperialism, as manifested in its domination of the Delian League and its demands for annual tribute, had simply been replaced by Spartan imperialism.

In 399 BCE, a new king was chosen in Sparta. Agesilaus II (c. 444–360 BCE) distinguished himself by his forthrightness and piety and proved to be a major statesman and general. One of his first projects after becoming king was to go to the aid of the pro–Sparta Greek cities

*Agesilaus II, shown on the right in this 18th-century-CE illustration, was king of Sparta in the fourth century BCE. He conducted several successful campaigns against the Persians.*

381

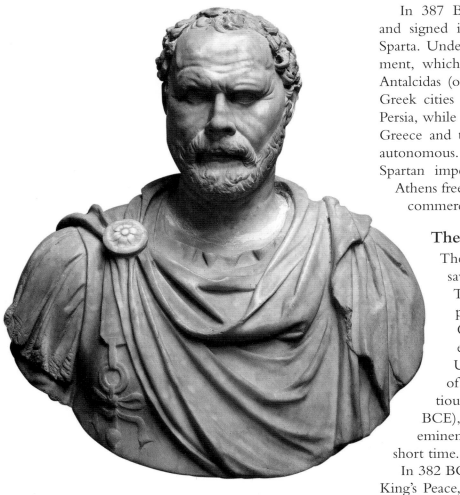

*The Athenian orator Demosthenes, depicted in this bust, warned his fellow Athenians of the threat posed by Philip II.*

In 387 BCE, Persia switched sides and signed its own peace treaty with Sparta. Under the terms of this settlement, which was called the Peace of Antalcidas (or the King's Peace), all the Greek cities in Anatolia were ceded to Persia, while the city-states of mainland Greece and the Aegean islands became autonomous. This treaty put an end to Spartan imperialist ambitions and left Athens free to develop its position as a commercial and cultural center.

## The rise of Thebes

The early fourth century BCE saw a new power arise. Thebes, a large city on the plain of Boeotia in central Greece, was known for the excellence of its army. Under the strong leadership of the charismatic and ambitious Epaminondas (c. 410–362 BCE), Thebes was to achieve preeminence in Greece for at least a short time.

In 382 BCE, despite the terms of the King's Peace, Sparta attacked and occupied Thebes. Thebes sought and received the support of Athens, and in 379 BCE, the Spartans were driven out. However, a full-scale war had started. Epaminondas was appointed army commander in 371 BCE. He introduced new infantry tactics that brought spectacular results at the Battle of Leuctra, fought the same year. It was traditional for hoplite commanders to put their strongest and most experienced soldiers on the right of their formations (to stop phalanxes from drifting to the right as soldiers sought protection behind their comrades' shields). At Leuctra, Epaminondas attacked in mass on the left. This surprise move allowed him to overwhelm the opposition.

After annihilating the Spartans at Leuctra, Epaminondas invaded the Peloponnese and annexed the regions of

in Anatolia. They were being harassed by Persian forces, so in 396 BCE, he took a large force to the coast of Anatolia to halt Persian raids. He campaigned around the Bosporus and the Meander River for the following two years. His success on the battlefield was an indication of the decline of the Persian Empire.

## The Corinthian War

On the mainland, a new threat to Sparta's dominance was looming. In 395 BCE, the cities of Athens, Argos, Corinth, and Thebes formed, with Persian support, an alliance against Sparta. Several battles were fought between Sparta and the coalition before Agesilaus was recalled from Anatolia to help deal with the situation. The conflict, called the Corinthian War, lasted eight years.

Arcadia and Messenia, freeing them from the yoke of Sparta. At a stroke, Thebes ended Sparta's dominance in Greece and took first place among the Greek city-states. However, the time of triumph for Thebes was short-lived. Alarmed by the emergence of this new rival, Sparta and Athens joined forces against the common enemy in 369 BCE. The new alliance engaged with the Theban army at the Battle of Mantinea in 362 BCE. Although the battle was indecisive, Epaminondas was killed, which put an end to the decade of glory enjoyed by Thebes.

## Macedonia

During the decade of Theban dominance (371–362 BCE), two Macedonian princes had been held as hostages in Thebes. In 359 BCE, one of these princes became Philip II, king of Macedon. Macedon lay just to the north of Thessaly, and during Philip's reign, it became a powerful state. The great Athenian orator Demosthenes understood that there was great danger lurking in the kingdom of Macedon and the wild surrounding region, and he incessantly warned the Athenian people of the threat of Philip. According to Demosthenes, Philip "was willing to sacrifice everything to gain fame and glory."

In his now famous oratories against Philip of Macedon (called the *Philippics*), Demosthenes spoke out with increasing vehemence against the danger posed by this military usurper from the north. When a rumor spread in Athens that Philip was seriously ill, Demosthenes railed at his fellow citizens: "Did Philip

*This coin bears the features of the Macedonian king Philip II. Philip's victory over a combined Greek army at Chaeronea changed the Mediterranean world.*

die? No, he is merely ill. And his illness is of no account, because even if Philip should die, your sluggishness would cause another Philip to rise up." In spite of the fact that the advancing Macedonian armies were uncomfortably close to the borders of Attica, the Greek city-states did not react.

Demosthenes' opponent was the orator Aeschines, who was acting as the spokesman for the pro-Macedonian party in the assembly. This party was in favor of a negotiated settlement with Philip. However, although Aeschines twice visited the Macedonian court, he had no success. In the end, Demosthenes succeeded in marginalizing the pro-Macedonian movement and then pushed for an alliance with Thebes. However, the alliance came too late, and it was not strong enough to stop Philip and the Macedonian army.

## Chaeronea

On August 7, 338 BCE, Philip of Macedon, with an army of 30,000 foot soldiers and 2,000 cavalry, defeated the smaller army of the Greek allies near Chaeronea on the plain of Boeotia. This battle gave Macedonia complete hegemony in Greece. Philip's young son Alexander played a key role in the Macedonians' victory. As Alexander the Great, he would later change the Greek world beyond all recognition.

**See also:**

The Age of Pericles (volume 3, page 340) • Macedon and Alexander the Great (volume 3, page 384) • Sparta and Athens (volume 2, page 258)

# MACEDON AND ALEXANDER THE GREAT

**A**lexander the Great was one of the greatest military leaders that the world has ever known. Building on the great military successes of his father, Philip II, Alexander created an empire that covered the entire eastern Mediterranean world.

The young Macedonian king Alexander crossed the Dardanelles in 334 BCE. He was scarcely 22 years old, and his aim was to conquer Persia and the whole of Asia. By the time he succumbed to fever at age 33, he had succeeded in moving the frontier of his empire 3,000 miles (4,800 km) east to the borders of India, subduing tens of millions of people along the way. However, his empire was to be short-lived—within a few years of his death, his generals had divided the vast territory among themselves.

## Early life

Alexander was born in 356 BCE in Pella, the capital of Macedonia. He was the son of Macedonia's king Philip II (ruled 359–336 BCE) and Olympias, a princess of Epirus, whom Philip had met when he was being initiated into the local religious mysteries of the island of Samothrace. When Alexander reached his teens, Philip sent for the Athenian philosopher Aristotle to teach his son rhetoric, philosophy, literature, and science. Alexander seems to have been an attentive student, and he remained in touch with Aristotle for the rest of his life.

According to the Greek biographer Plutarch, Alexander inherited a love of medicine from his tutor. The king would prescribe treatment and medication to his friends when they were ill. Plutarch goes on to describe how Alexander was an avid reader and would go to bed with a copy of the *Iliad*, which he would place next to his dagger under his headrest. On his Asian campaign, he ordered his treasurer Harpalus to send him books. Among the works that he received were Philistus's history of Sicily and the plays of Euripides, Sophocles, and Aeschylus.

Alexander was only 14 years old when he got his first taste of power and command. When his father went away on campaign and left him in charge of Macedon, Alexander successfully fought off an attack by a tribe of Thracians. Two years later, at the age of 16, he was given a command at the Battle of Chaeronea, where the Macedonians defeated the Greek forces.

## Ascent to the throne

Philip II was assassinated in the summer of 336 BCE. The reason has never been clearly established. The Persians may have been behind it, or even Alexander himself, who was not on the best of terms with his father. Whatever the truth of the matter, Alexander ascended the throne and had the alleged conspirators summarily executed.

Before his assassination, Philip had been preparing to invade Anatolia (present-day Turkey) via the Dardanelles. Alexander was anxious to continue this

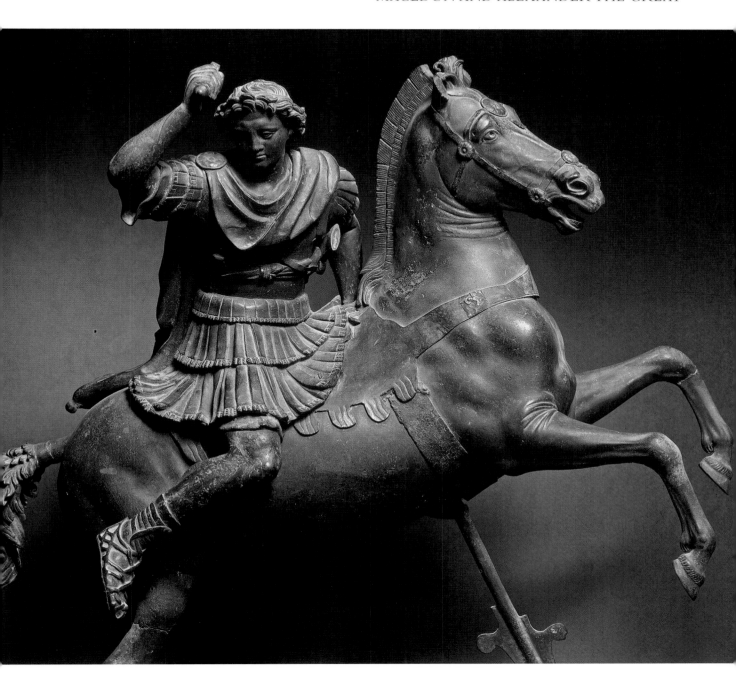

mission against the region's Persian-held cities, but before he could embark on the campaign, he had to deal with troubles closer to home. In Thessaly, leaders of an independence movement had taken over the government. Alexander threw them out and reasserted Macedonian rule. By the end of the summer, Alexander had been elected leader of the Corinthian League (a military alliance created by his father), although he could not count on the support of the Greek city-states south of Thermopylae.

The following year, Alexander crossed the northern border to quell rebellious Thracians. The successful campaign lasted for five months and took him as far as the Danube River. On his return, he took only a week to subdue yet another rebellion, this time by the Illyrians.

*This statue depicts Alexander the Great on horseback. Alexander's Companion cavalry was a key component of his army.*

385

*This medallion bears a depiction of Philip II of Macedonia, the father of Alexander the Great. Philip greatly enlarged his kingdom through a series of military campaigns in the early years of his reign.*

After he put down the Illyrian rebellion, Alexander was forced to confront yet another insurrection, one by the city of Thebes, located on the plain of Boeotia. The revolt, supported by a number of other Greek cities, was incited by the orator Demosthenes and funded by Persian gold. The rebels spread the rumor that Alexander was dead and then attacked the Macedonian garrison occupying the citadel. Hearing this news, Alexander moved his army rapidly southward in forced marches. One morning, the Thebans were alarmed to see that the king they had presumed dead was outside their walls. The Macedonians took the city by storm, razing it and spar–

## PHILIP OF MACEDON

Philip of Macedon, the father of Alexander, was born around 382 BCE, the third son of King Amyntas of Macedonia. When his brother Perdiccas was killed in a battle against the Illyrians in 359 BCE, Philip became king at around the age of 23. Philip was a shrewd diplomat and an inspired military commander who was to transform his hitherto insignificant kingdom into the most powerful Greek state.

At that time, Macedon was beset by enemies, and one of Philip's priorities on acceding to the throne was to reorganize his army into a more efficient fighting force. He introduced rigorous new training and refined the phalanx formation. Under Philip, the soldiers that made up the phalanx were armed with metal-tipped pikes around 16 feet (4.9 m) long. He also

incorporated equipment for siege warfare, such as catapults and siege towers.

With his revitalized army, Philip embarked on a 20-year campaign of warfare and diplomacy that was to make him master of the Greek world. In 357 BCE, he married Olympias, a princess of Epirus, and a year later, she bore him a son whom they named Alexander. In 338 BCE, having subjugated all his non-Greek neighbors, Philip invaded mainland Greece and defeated the combined forces of Athens and Thebes at the Battle of Chaeronea. Once Greece was his, Philip planned to invade Anatolia and conquer the Persian-held cities. However, before his preparations were much advanced, Philip was assassinated, leaving the throne of Macedon and the conquest of Persia to his son, Alexander.

# THE PHALANX

Much of the deadly efficiency of Alexander's army depended on the phalanx, which had been restyled by his father, Philip II of Macedon. The phalanx was made up of around 9,000 infantrymen, often drawn up in 256-man squares, 16 men wide and 16 men deep. The weapon of the phalanx was the *sarissa*, a long, heavy pike that measured around 16 feet (4.9 m). These weapons were held horizontally by the first few rows, making a wall of sharp points that stretched 10 feet (3 m) or more ahead of the advancing phalanx. Because the infantry of opposing armies tended to be armed with spears no more than 8 feet (2.4 m) long, the Macedonian phalanx had an immediate advantage.

An advancing phalanx presented a deadly wall of metal spikes and was a formidable fighting force. While the *sarissas* of the leading rows were inflicting damage on their opponents, casualties within the phalanx were immediately replaced by men from the rear. However, a moving phalanx was effective only on level ground and was vulnerable on its flanks, which had to be protected by cavalry or light infantry such as slingers. For this reason, the usual function of the phalanx was defensive—while it stood its ground as the enemy attacked, the cavalry could harass their adversaries on the flanks.

The phalanx was a flexible unit that could, if necessary, assume different shapes—such as a square, a rectangle, or even a wedge or arrowhead shape. Because the *sarissa* required both hands to hold it, each soldier wore his circular shield on a neckstrap. When in battle, the shield was brought around to the front of the body. Each soldier also wore a helmet and greaves.

*This artist's illustration depicts a Macedonian phalanx about to engage with the enemy. The front three rows of the square hold their pikes horizontally. The soldiers in the rows farther back hold them at an angle, ready to replace any fallen comrades.*

# THE EMPIRE OF ALEXANDER THE GREAT

**KEY**

Empire of Alexander at its greatest extent

✕  Major battle

ing only the temples and the house of the famous Greek poet Pindar. Of the surviving inhabitants, some 8,000 were sold into slavery. The speed and severity of this retaliation left such an impression on the other rebellious Greek cities that they surrendered almost immediately and were treated with comparative leniency by Alexander.

## Into Asia

Leaving his general Antipater as regent of Macedonia and Greece, Alexander was free to embark on the long-delayed Asian campaign. He set out with a formidable army that comprised 30,000 foot soldiers and some 5,000 horsemen. These cavalry units were the core units of the force and were composed mainly of Macedonians and Thessalians. There were also many

Macedonians among the infantry, but at least half of the footsoldiers were mercenaries drawn from the rest of the Greek world, from Thrace, and from regions farther north.

Alexander was also surrounded by his personal retinue, called the *hetairoi*, or Companions. This *hetairoi* squadron of 1,500 men was mainly drawn from the Macedonian aristocracy. They answered directly to Alexander and, wherever he was and whatever he did, his *hetairoi* were always near. The king regarded the members as his friends and allowed them liberties not granted to others.

Alexander did not have much difficulty in assembling his army. Since the peace forged by him and his father in Greece, there had been a much reduced demand for mercenaries. Serving as a mercenary was a popular occupation. Although the soldier had to provide his own equipment, military service provided pay and a share of any booty won. Mercenaries were accustomed to serving on the side that offered the greatest reward. Many Greek soldiers had already crossed the Aegean Sea to join Persian troop contingents. In every one of his battles against the Persians, Alexander faced opposing Greek mercenaries. Many of them defected to his army—not through patriotism, but because they expected higher earnings.

Alexander's Companions, the army's elite horsemen, were highly skilled riders and were armed with lances and short swords. They trained intensively so their horses would be manageable in battle. Alexander almost invariably led the charge of his Companion cavalry himself, and these attacks generally inflicted great damage on the enemy.

The main foot soldiers were used in a phalanx (see box, page 387), a formation that had been in use long before the time of Philip and Alexander. However, the Macedonians adapted it by using far longer spears than their predecessors. If the formation became confused, all was lost; it was impossible to restore the original order in the heat of battle. Generally, the phalanx was able to resist a frontal attack by cavalry but not one from the side. For this reason, the phalanx was always placed at the center of the battle formation, with the cavalry and more mobile infantry at its flanks. Alexander exploited the flexibility of this army to great advantage, and it brought him victory after victory.

## The Battle of Granicus River

In the spring of 334 BCE, Alexander led his army of 35,000 Macedonians and Greeks across the Dardanelles and into Anatolia. At the Granicus River in northwestern Anatolia, he attacked an army of 40,000 Persians and Greeks. Alexander won the battle and reputedly lost only 110 soldiers of his own. The road to Anatolia lay open.

The victory at Granicus River had a serious effect on Persian morale. When

*Alexander (left, on horseback) leads his forces against those of Darius III (in chariot) at the Battle of Issus. This Roman mosaic was found in the city of Pompeii and dates to the fourth century BCE.*

**Alexander Cuts the Gordian Knot,** *by Jean-Simon Berhtélemy, dates to either the late 18th or early 19th century CE. An ancient prophecy foretold that anyone who undid the knot would rule Asia.*

Alexander's army approached the Persian government center of Sardis, which had long been able to withstand attack, the governor walked out through the gate to surrender. One by one, the Greek colonies of Ionia fell to Macedonian hands, and it took Alexander barely a year to subdue the whole of Anatolia.

After the Persian king Xerxes died in 424 BCE, the kingdom of Persia had gone into decline. Under a succession of ineffective kings, the provincial governors had divided Persia into a large number of semi-independent principalities. Artaxerxes, king of Persia from 358 to 338 BCE, had restored his authority in the cities of Susa and Persepolis with brutal force, so it is possible that many Persians regarded Alexander's arrival as a liberation.

## The Gordian knot

On his route of conquest, Alexander passed through Gordium (the capital of Phrygia), which was home to an ancient legend. According to Greek mythology, Gordius, a Phrygian peasant, had been made king because he fulfilled a prophecy that said that the first person to enter the town driving a wagon must be made ruler. The grateful king dedicated his wagon to Zeus, tying it with a complex knot in a grove in the god's temple. The knot was so difficult that no one could undo it—it was said that anyone who could untie it would rule all of Asia. When he was told this story, Alexander unsheathed his sword and simply sliced through the knot. This act gave rise to the expression "cutting the Gordian knot," meaning to find a swift and imaginative solution to a difficult problem. For this act, Alexander was rewarded with enough booty to cover his campaign expenses.

Carrying on south to Syria, the Macedonians encountered a large Persian army, commanded by King Darius III himself. At the ensuing Battle of Issus, the Persians outnumbered the

Macedonians by almost two to one, yet the result was a catastrophic defeat for the Persians. When Alexander and his cavalry penetrated the Persian infantry, Darius turned and fled, with much of his army following. Alexander captured Darius's wife, mother, and children, who had been left behind in the Persian army's camp. However, Alexander ordered that they be treated with the respect normally accorded to royalty. He was already beginning to make efforts to placate conquered peoples in order to build a socially integrated empire.

## Phoenicia

After the Battle of Issus, Alexander carried on down the coast of Syria and Phoenicia. His object was to capture all of the ports of the eastern Mediterranean, thereby cutting the Persians off from their naval bases. Alexander encountered little resistance; only the well-fortified Phoenician seaport of Tyre put up a fight. Although its rulers were willing to acknowledge Alexander as king, they were not prepared to let him and his army enter the island on which the city lay. A prolonged siege of seven months followed, but finally, in 332 BCE, Alexander seized the city and razed it in a bloodbath. Any surviving citizens, including all the women and children, were sold into slavery.

After the fall of Tyre, Darius offered all his lands up to the Euphrates River, his daughter in marriage, and a large dowry in exchange for peace with Alexander. As a guarantee of his good intentions, Darius offered to send his son as a hostage. However, Alexander replied

*This silver coin, which bears a portrait of Alexander, was issued during the reign of Seleucus I, several decades after the death of Alexander.*

that he already had whatever Darius could offer and that he would marry his daughter regardless of her father's permission. Alexander also said that he would come to take what he considered his, but not immediately.

Alexander continued down the Mediterranean coast to the fortress at Gaza, which also offered resistance. It took a long siege before the city was taken, and because Alexander was injured in the course of the siege, he exacted a terrible revenge. Jerusalem, however, surrendered without a single blow being exchanged—the high priest came out in full regalia to welcome the conqueror and his army.

## Egypt

Later that same year, 332 BCE, Alexander led his army across the Sinai Peninsula and into Egypt, where the Persian governor surrendered without a fight. Alexander was welcomed everywhere as a liberator, and he was installed as the new pharaoh. Alexander founded a new city on the coast next to the mouth of the Nile River. Named Alexandria, the city was destined to become the commercial and cultural center of the Greek world (see box, page 392).

During the summer of 331 BCE, Alexander made a pilgrimage to the oracle of Amon-Re, the Egyptian god of the sun, at the Siwa Oasis in the Libyan desert. Around this time, Alexander had begun to entertain the notion that he was descended from the gods, and the Egyptians, who had made him their pharaoh, did not attempt to dissuade him from the idea; all Egyptian pharaohs were considered to be the sons of Amon-Re. The oracle apparently confirmed his

# THE CITY OF ALEXANDRIA

Founded by Alexander the Great in 332 BCE, Alexandria was designed to be a model city that would reflect the splendor of its founder. It was probably originally conceived as a military stronghold and naval base, but it rapidly became the trading and administrative center of Egypt under the Greeks. Situated on the Mediterranean coast just west of the Nile Delta, it extended for around 4 miles (6.5 km) along the coast and around 1 to 2 miles (2–3 km) inland. Its streets were laid out in a grid pattern, with two wide main avenues where many of the most important commercial and cultural buildings were found. At its southern end, an isthmus projected into the Mediterranean Sea and separated two great harbors. In 280 BCE, a lighthouse around 460 feet (140 m) high was built at the mouth of one of the harbors. It has since disappeared, but in its time, the lighthouse was counted as one of the seven wonders of the world.

After Alexander's death in 323 BCE, the city came under the control of the Egyptian Ptolemaic dynasty and continued to flourish. Its two big harbors made it an important center for Mediterranean trade. Alexandria exported various products manufactured by Alexandrian craftspeople, including linen, papyrus, and precious metalwork. It was also an important transit port for Egyptian grain and wares from India, Arabia, and even more distant countries. These wares arrived by way of the Red Sea and the caravan routes.

Within 100 years of its founding, Alexandria had become the leading city of the world and the center of Greek cultural life. Its great library housed hundreds of thousands of books and attracted many scholars and poets, including Theocritus, Apollonius, and Callimachus. Another great center of learning and research was the Museum, next to the royal palace of the Ptolemies. The Museum was both a temple of the Muses and a research institute where scholars and artists could devote themselves to learning at the ruler's expense.

*Alexandria, shown in this undated modern illustration, was perfectly situated for trade.*

divine lineage, and because the Greeks identified Amon-Re with Zeus, Alexander proclaimed himself to be a son of Zeus. The Greeks had no difficulty with this concept, involving as it did a young king with military achievements so remarkable as to appear superhuman. Divine or not, Alexander was a great man, and most Greeks and Egyptians were happy to treat him as a god.

## The Battle of Gaugamela

Once he had secured the Mediterranean coast (he had also captured Cyrene, capital of the kingdom of Cyrenaica on the north African coast), Alexander turned his attention north and east. In the late summer of 331 BCE, he retraced his steps across the Sinai Peninsula and then proceeded up through Palestine to Babylon. He had with him an army of 40,000 infantry and 7,000 cavalry, and after crossing the Euphrates and Tigris rivers, Alexander found Darius waiting for him with a far larger army.

The two forces engaged near the town of Gaugamela in northern Mesopotamia on October 1, 331 BCE. In spite of the disparity in numbers, and the fact that the Persian army included an Indian contingent with elephants, the Macedonians were again victorious, although they suffered heavy losses. Once again, Darius fled from the battlefield, taking refuge in the mountains to the northeast.

Alexander turned south and entered Babylon, which surrendered without a fight. From there, he continued eastward into Persia, conquering the royal city of

*This relief sculpture depicts the Persian king Darius I. Darius's great palace of Persepolis was destroyed by Alexander.*

Susa (which held the treasury of the Persian Empire), the capital Persepolis, and Pasagardae. The splendid palace at Persepolis, built by Darius I as a symbol of the might and wealth of the Persian Empire, was looted by the army and set on fire by Alexander, possibly in a fit of drunkenness. It burned to the ground.

Alexander was lord of all Persia—Darius had essentially forfeited the

## A PORTRAIT OF ALEXANDER

Alexander was of medium height, with fair hair and a pale complexion. He grew up believing he would achieve greatness (his mother encouraged him to believe he was not actually Philip's son but a son of the god Zeus), and from an early age, he yearned to explore the world. He excelled at all martial skills but was not keen on any other sports apart from hunting. He became a heavy drinker and was capable of ungovernable rages and great cruelty. He had a lifelong passionate relationship with Hephaestion, a young Macedonian aristocrat, and when Hephaestion died of a fever in 324 BCE, Alexander was prostrated with grief. He organized a stunningly expensive royal funeral in Babylon for his friend and built an extravagant monument to him.

throne. In the summer of 330 BCE, Darius was murdered at the instigation of a group of satraps (local governors). One of them—Bessus—then proclaimed himself king. Alexander branded the satraps as regicides and usurpers, but Bessus unleashed a popular war, forcing the Macedonians and the Persians into yet another conflict. Bessus was eventually betrayed, taken by Alexander, and executed as a traitor.

## Central Asia and India

In 329 BCE, Alexander set out on a new campaign to complete his conquest of the eastern Persian Empire, including the provinces of western India. Over the following two years, he broke the last traces of resistance in central Asia, extending his realm to encompass Media and Parthia (present-day Iran, Afghanistan, and Baluchistan) and Bactria and Sogdiana (present-day Turkmenistan).

In 327 BCE, Alexander led his army over the dangerous pass through the Hindu Kush mountains to reach the Indus Valley. There, in 326 BCE, he encountered the Indian king Porus, whose considerable army contained a mighty contingent of elephants. The Battle of Hydaspes was fought in torrential monsoon rains, and Alexander was once again victorious. He captured Porus and made him the local governor under Macedonian rule.

Despite their successes, Alexander's troops had begun to grow unhappy with their lot. It was rumored that they still had far to go, even that Alexander's aim was to conquer the whole world. In the fall of 326 BCE, the troops mutinied and refused to proceed any further. They had been on campaign for eight years and wanted to go home. Alexander was forced to compromise; he could not continue without an army. He abandoned the idea of conquering the rest of India. Instead, he had a fleet built and sailed down the Indus River

Alexander reached the mouth of the river in 325 BCE. From there, the fleet continued by sea to the Persian Gulf, while Alexander and the army marched west by land along the arid coastline. The fleet was supposed to sail parallel to the army's line of travel, to keep it supplied with food and water, but because the ships were unable to sail close to land against the prevailing winds, the army was forced to forage for supplies. Because

*Alexander the Great and Hephaestion hunt a lion in this contemporary mosaic from the Macedonian palace at Pella. Hephaestion was a boyhood friend of Alexander's who served with him on many of his campaigns; he was also possibly his lover.*

the army needed a daily supply of 1,190,000 gallons (720,000 l) of water and 250 tons (225 tonnes) of cereals to survive, many troops perished. Alexander lost more men on this march than in he did in all his battles combined.

## Uniting the empire

In 324 BCE, Alexander returned to Susa to attend to affairs of state. In an effort to reconcile the conquered and the conquerors, he organized a funeral for Darius (the last of the Achaemenids) so that he was buried with his forefathers with due ceremony. Alexander adopted Persian customs, wearing the vestments and insignia of the "king of kings" on all ceremonial occasions. He arranged a mass marriage ceremony of Macedonian men with Persian wives, at which he himself married Barsine, the daughter of Darius. He also appointed Persians to important offices and drafted thousands of young Persians into his army.

These actions showed that Alexander intended to create a mixed Macedonian-Persian elite that would hold his empire together, but they resulted in considerable tension between Alexander and his Macedonian entourage, particularly his *hetairoi*. When the new Persian troops were called up at the same time that Macedonian veterans were dismissed, the veterans mutinied. However, Alexander still had enough influence to effect a reconciliation with the rebels. At a celebratory banquet for the entire army, he openly prayed to the gods for "unity and equally shared rule" between Macedonians and Persians.

*The so-called Alexander sarcophagus is decorated with scenes from the emperor's life, even though it does not actually contain his body. The sarcophagus was made in the fourth century BCE.*

## Final days

In the spring of 323 BCE, Alexander transferred to Babylon, where he took up his quarters in the palace of Nebuchadnezzar. Soon after his arrival, Alexander came down with a fever, an illness that was probably aggravated by heavy drinking. He died ten days later, on June 10. He was 33 years old. Alexander bequeathed his empire "to the strongest," thereby setting off a power struggle that was to last for 50 years.

**See also:**

After Alexander (volume 3, page 396) • The Persians (volume 2, page 232)

# AFTER ALEXANDER

After the death of Alexander in 323 BCE, several empires rose to prominence. The Ptolemaic dynasty took control of Egypt, the Antigonids rose to power in Macedonia, and the Seleucids took over the area that had formerly belonged to the Persians.

When Alexander the Great died at age 33 in 323 BCE, he left behind a power vacuum. The ensuing struggle among his generals was to result in the eventual breakup of his mighty empire into three main kingdoms.

## The age of the diadochs

Alexander's first wife, Roxana, did not give birth to their son, also called Alexander, until four weeks after the king's death. The only other person with any claim to the throne was the 35-year-old Aridaeus, an illegitimate son of Philip II, who was rumored to suffer from both physical and mental illness. Nevertheless, both the newborn Alexander and his uncle Aridaeus were immediately invested with imperial titles—Alexander IV and Philip III. Since neither of them was in a position to exercise power, it fell into the hands of the imperial regent, Perdiccas, who divided the empire among the commanders of Alexander's army. These commanders are known as the *diadochoi* (successors), or diadochs.

For a time, while each diadoch attempted to secure for himself as much land and wealth as possible, a precarious unity was preserved in the empire, but the diadochs soon fell into open conflict. Years of war ensued, many of them marked by the formation of fresh coalitions. In 317 BCE, Aridaeus was murdered. After the 13-year-old Alexander met a similar fate in 310 BCE, there was no longer any lawful successor to stand in the way of the diadochs' ambitions.

## Ptolemy and Egypt

One of the kingdoms that was to emerge from the breakup of Alexander's empire was a new, Greek-influenced Egypt, ruled by the diadoch Ptolemy (c. 367–283 BCE). Ptolemy came from an aristocratic Macedonian family and had grown up in the court of Philip II, becoming a friend of the king's young son, Alexander. When Alexander embarked on his Asian campaign, Ptolemy accompanied him as a general in his army. Ptolemy was later appointed satrap (governor) of Egypt.

After Alexander's death, Ptolemy was confirmed as diadoch in charge of Egypt and Libya, and he used the position as a power base. For almost 20 years, he battled the other diadochs, consolidating and expanding his realm. He successfully fended off invasions of Egypt and the island of Rhodes and annexed Cyprus, Palestine, and Cyrenaica. In 305 BCE, he proclaimed himself king of Egypt, taking the title Ptolemy I.

*This Roman wall painting depicts Antigonus Gonatas, who helped establish the Antigonid dynasty in Macedonia.*

*This coin bears the portrait of Ptolemy I. A former general in Alexander's army, Ptolemy crowned himself king of Egypt in 305 BCE.*

culture. The new king built a famous library and museum that attracted and supported Greek scholars and artists from all over the Greek world.

Ptolemy I died around 283 BCE, having established a dynasty that was to rule Egypt until the arrival of the Romans in 32 BCE.

## Antigonus and son

Antigonus was another important general in Alexander's army. He was nicknamed Monophthalmos (One-Eye), the result of his having lost an eye in battle. Antigonus was already an old man—almost 60 years old—at the time of Alexander's death. For the previous 10 years, he had been governor of the recently conquered Phrygia, ruling the territory while the king went on to other conquests.

In 321 BCE, having been made commander in chief in Asia, Antigonus joined forces with his son Demetrius Poliorcetes (Taker of Cities), so-called for his skill in laying sieges. Together they hoped to preserve the unity of the empire, but they almost immediately found themselves in conflict with the other diadochs. Initially, they were very successful in battle, and in 306 BCE, they proclaimed themselves joint kings as Alexander's successors, ruling a huge region centered around western Asia

Taking up residence in his capital city, Alexandria, Ptolemy set about expanding the might and wealth of his kingdom. He improved the administrative system and established a system of land registration to simplify the collection of taxes. He also expanded Alexandria itself, making it the largest Greek settlement in the known world.

Ptolemy succeeded in having his friend Alexander's body brought to Egypt. Although it was known that Alexander would have preferred the Siwa Oasis as his final resting place, the funeral took place in Alexandria. The body was placed in a golden coffin and given divine honors.

In 285 BCE, Ptolemy abdicated in favor of his son, Ptolemy II. It was Ptolemy II who was to make Alexandria an unparalleled center of learning and

Five years later, in 301 BCE, Antigonus and Demetrius were forced to defend their territory against a coalition of the other diadochs (now also calling themselves kings) at the Battle of Ipsus. Antigonus, now 80, was killed, but Demetrius escaped to Greece. There, he succeeded in conquering Macedonia and much of mainland Greece, but in 286 BCE, while on a campaign in Anatolia, he was captured and imprisoned by the diadoch Seleucus. Demetrius died in prison in 283 BCE.

## THE HELLENISTIC WORLD IN 270 BCE

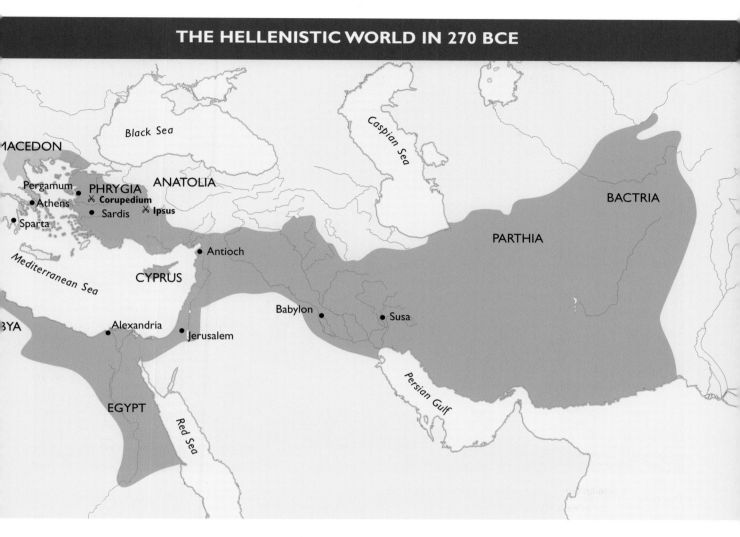

Black Sea

Caspian Sea

MACEDON

Pergamum

PHRYGIA    ANATOLIA

Athens    ✗ Corupedium

Sparta    ✗ Ipsus

Sardis

BACTRIA

PARTHIA

Mediterranean Sea    CYPRUS    Antioch

LIBYA    Alexandria    Babylon    Susa

Jerusalem

EGYPT    Persian Gulf

Red Sea

## KEY

Seleucid kingdom

Ptolemaic kingdom

Macedonian kingdom

✗    Major battle

Demetrius's son, Antigonus Gonatas, regained possession of the Macedonian throne around 272 BCE, and his descendants—the Antigonids—remained in power until the Romans put an end to their dynasty.

## The Seleucids

The Seleucid Empire was the largest of the kingdoms that resulted from the division of Alexander's domains. It was founded by Seleucus, one of the diadochs who rose to power after Alexander's death. Born around 358 BCE, Seleucus was, like Ptolemy, the son of a Macedonian aristocrat. He was roughly the same age as Alexander and probably his friend. He accompanied the young king on his Persian campaign and, after Alexander's death, was appointed governor of Babylon.

Having secured Babylon and the regions farther east, Seleucus gradually expanded his influence to the west. In Syria, he built himself a new capital city, Antioch, which was to become the most important metropolis in Asia. In 281 BCE, Seleucus met the diadoch Lysimachus at the Battle of Corupedium near Sardis and defeated him, thereby securing Anatolia for himself. Because Lysimachus (who was killed in the fighting) had been the king of Macedonia, Seleucus tried to secure that territory. However, before he could achieve this aim, he was assassinated.

*Pompey's Pillar, built in the third century CE, is one of the most famous monuments in Alexandria. Alexandria was the capital of Egypt during the Ptolemaic period.*

## JUDAS MACCABAEUS

The most famous opponent of the Seleucids is probably the Jewish guerrilla fighter Judas Maccabaeus. Palestine was seized from the Ptolemies by the Seleucid king Antiochus III in 198 BCE. In 168 BCE, Antiochus IV outlawed Judaism, ordering the worship of Greek gods and persecuting anyone who remained true to the Jewish religion and culture.

Mattathias, patriarch of the priestly Hasmonaean family, objected to this edict and killed both a government official and a Jew who had complied with the order. In 167 BCE, Mattathias fled to the mountains with a loyal band of Jews, initiating a lengthy revolt against the Seleucids. After he died, his son Judas Maccabaeus (The Hammer) took command of the rebellion, defeating much larger Syrian armies in 166 and 165 BCE and capturing Jerusalem. He restored Jewish rites to the temple in Jerusalem in December 165 BCE, an event that is commemorated by the Jewish festival of Hanukkah. For the next 80 years, the Jews in Syria were virtually an independent nation.

Seleucus had carved out an enormous empire, one that almost rivaled Alexander's in size. He was succeeded by his son, Antiochus I. The Seleucid dynasty was to survive for more than two hundred years.

The people who lived within the boundaries of the Seleucid Empire spoke many languages and adhered to many different ways of life. The empire never became truly integrated, and under Seleucus's successors, it gradually crumbled away. In central Asia, Bactria made itself virtually independent, while in northern Persia, the warlike Parthians roamed at will, ultimately conquering many of the eastern provinces. Other usurpers set up their own kingdoms in imperial territory. One such state was Pergamum, on the Aegean coast, which rebelled against Seleucid rule to become the leading city of Anatolia and an important hub of Greek culture.

## Antipater and the Lamian War

Antipater (c. 397–319 BCE) was a trusted friend of Philip II and Alexander the Great. When Alexander embarked on his Persian campaign, Antipater was left behind to act as his regent in Macedonia and Greece. As soon as news of Alexander's death reached Greece in 323 BCE, Athens and several other states rebelled. The insurrection was spurred on by the oratory of Demosthenes, who had long led Athenian opposition to Macedonia. Antipater acted promptly to put down the revolt.

The conflict between Antipater and the Greek states was called the Lamian War. The Athenians were backed by the Aetolian League, an alliance based in the mountainous region of Aetolia. At first, the rebels were successful, but Antipater eventually crushed them at the Battle of Crannon in 322 BCE.

Antipater demanded that the Athenians hand over the rebel leaders, including

*This bust depicts the diadoch Seleucus I. In the decades following Alexander the Great's death, Seleucus gained control of much of the eastern part of Alexander's empire.*

Demosthenes, and the Athenian assembly condemned the rebels to death. Demosthenes managed to escape to the island of Calauria, where he took poison rather than surrender.

Antipater's next battle was with his own countryman, the Macedonian general Partakes, who challenged his authority. Antipater won this struggle easily—Partakes was killed in 321 BCE. Antipater was then confirmed as supreme regent of Macedonia and charged with the care of Alexander's children. On Antipater's death in 319 BCE, the regency passed to Polypechon, but he was swiftly replaced by Antipater's son Cassander, who seized control. Continued infighting between the diadochs led eventually to Antigonus

Gonatas becoming the king of Macedon in 272 BCE. He established a dynasty that was to last for more than a hundred years.

By the early third century BCE, therefore, Alexander's entire empire had been broadly divided into three much smaller empires. Macedonia was ruled by the Antigonid dynasty, solidly established in their homeland. Outside Macedonia, their position was less strong, but their sphere of influence extended from present-day Bulgaria to the Peloponnese. Egypt was ruled by the Ptolemies, who gradually relinquished their possessions beyond its borders. The Seleucid dynasty held the region that had originally stretched from the Aegean Sea in the west to the Indus River in the east. However, over the years, the eastern boundary was gradually eroded and receded westward. Although the diadoch dynasties lived in continual conflict, no one empire was able to achieve dominance. The division of power remained unsettled until the advent of the Rome Empire.

## Hellenism

The campaigns of Alexander the Great had far-reaching consequences that were not only political but also social and cultural. In his epic progress of conquest across Asia, he had established many new cities and populated them with Greek veterans from his army. Those cities became oases of Greek language and culture in the middle of an Oriental culture, which gave rise to the concept of Hellenism, a term used to describe the unprecedented spread of Greek culture

*Judas Maccabaeus led a Jewish rebellion against the Seleucid Empire, capturing the city of Jerusalem.*

in the east in the period between the death of Alexander and the beginning of the Christian era.

Alexander had founded cities as far away as Uzbekistan and Kashmir, leaving the new cities as small, isolated islands of Greek civilization in an enormous sea of local culture. However, the new Greek cities were not modeled on the old idea of a city-state ruled by its citizens. That concept had no place in Alexander's empire; these cities were ruled by a distant king. Greek was generally used as the common language in large parts of the Hellenistic empires, without wholly replacing Aramaic, which had played a similar role in the Persian Empire. In spite of this unity of language, Greek culture had little effect on the indigenous population. In most cases, the Greeks and the native inhabitants existed side by side, with little interaction between them.

Although the old Greek gods were worshipped in the new Greek cities, they faced fierce competition from the non-Greek gods that surrounded them. Many of these other gods were messianic (saviors or deliverers) with cults of an ecstatic nature. Similar Greek cults, especially Dionysiac cults, also flourished at this time. The cult of the ruler derived strength from the popularity of the messianic gods: often, he too was regarded as a savior or messiah.

The Greeks did not automatically adopt foreign gods—the gods first had to be adapted to Greek tastes, which was done through a process of syncretism. Syncretism occurs when deities merge by assuming one another's characteristics. In this way, the Egyptian god Amon-Re and the Syrian god Baal became identified with Zeus.

## Cleomenes

While changes were occurring in western Asia, social conditions were deteriorating on many parts of the Greek mainland. In Sparta, there were fewer than 1,000 Spartans left with full citizenship

rights, and most of them were living below subsistence level. All the wealth was in the hands of a select few. In the last half of the third century BCE, when the situation was ripe for revolution, a reforming leader emerged: Cleomenes.

Cleomenes III became one of the two kings of Sparta in 235 BCE. He was determined to introduce new policies to redress the inequalities in Spartan society. After ridding himself of his political enemies, he took the radical course of canceling all debts and dividing the land into equal parcels, which he distributed among the citizens. At the same time, he granted full citizenship to several thousand of the *perioikoi* (original inhabitants). The revolutionary ideas of Cleomenes spread, and in many Greek states, a cry arose for debts to be canceled and land to be redistributed.

Cleomenes also attempted to restore Sparta's military prestige by going to war with the Achaean League, an alliance of city-states under the leadership of Aratus of Sicyon. Aratus was deeply opposed to the revolutionary ideas fanned by Cleomenes, and in order to ensure his success in battle against the Spartans, he called on the help of Macedon. Cleomenes was defeated, and his reforms were dismantled. The king fled to Alexandria, where he died in 219 BCE.

Roughly 20 years later, the radical ideas of Cleomenes resurfaced during the brutal reign of the Spartan tyrant Nabis (ruled 207-192 BCE). Nabis reintroduced Cleomenes' system, even going so far as to free the slaves, but his rule came to an end when he was betrayed by his allies during a war against Rome. His death marked the end of Sparta's days as a major power.

**See also:**

Macedon and Alexander the Great (volume 3, page 384) • Sparta and Athens (volume 2, page 258)

# THE GREEK LEGACY

## TIME LINE

**332 BCE**
Alexander the Great founds city of Alexandria.

**c. 308 BCE**
Zeno of Cyprus begins giving lectures in Athens; his teachings form basis of school of philosophy known as Stoicism.

**c. 300 BCE**
Ptolemy I expands Temple of the Muses in Alexandria to establish center for arts and sciences; Euclid writes *Elements*.

**c. 275 BCE**
Aristarchus of Samos suggests Earth orbits around sun, instead of sun orbiting around Earth; radical theory rejected.

**c. 250 BCE**
Aristotle studies at Museum in Alexandria before returning to native Syracuse; he formulates concept of specific gravity.

The ancient Greeks made profound and far-reaching contributions to the worlds of literature, science, and philosophy. Their discoveries and achievements became the building blocks for generations of later scholars and artists.

Many of the cultural achievements associated with ancient Greece took place not in Greece itself but in the Greek outpost of Alexandria in Egypt. The city was founded by Alexander the Great in 332 BCE. When he left Egypt to go on a campaign, Alexander left one of his generals, Ptolemy, in charge of the province. On Alexander's death in 323 BCE, Ptolemy effectively became the ruler of Egypt. He crowned himself king of the country in 305 BCE.

From the very beginning of his reign, Ptolemy encouraged Greek scholars and philosophers to congregate at his court in Alexandria. When Demetrius of Phaleron was banished from Athens, he took refuge in Alexandria and suggested that Ptolemy should establish a center of study dedicated to the Muses (see box, page 412). The center would allow scholars to pursue their studies in all the arts and sciences. Ptolemy happily agreed to the idea.

## The first museum

The Temple of the Muses was expanded to make it a true academy of literature and the sciences. The Greeks knew the temple as the Mouseion, although it is now known as the Museum—the origin of the word used today. Those who were appointed to work there became well-paid servants of the state and lived in the building. They were overseen by the director and chief priest.

Under Ptolemy's son, Ptolemy II (ruled 285–246 BCE), Alexandria became renowned as a center of arts and a magnet for scholars and poets, whom Ptolemy welcomed to his court. He increased his financial support for the Museum, which became a research center for the natural sciences and mathematics as well as an academy for more literary pursuits.

Most of the writers working at the Museum did not produce original work. Instead, they focused on collecting and preserving the literary works of the past. The versions of Homer's epic poems the *Iliad* and the *Odyssey* that exist today are essentially the work of Alexandrian scholars. The Museum's archivists collected manuscripts of literary texts attributed to Homer and then compiled them to produce new editions. Copies of these texts were widely sold and greatly prized for their authenticity.

The scholars also did invaluable work in the area of textual criticism, a discipline that had its beginnings in Alexandria. After scrutinizing all available manuscripts of a text, the scholars would

*This 15th-century-CE painting by Joos Van Gent depicts the astronomer Ptolemy of Alexandria.*

publish their own version of an ancient work, together with annotation. Crucial to this process of textual criticism were the resources provided by the great Library of Alexandria, which contained many thousands of handwritten scrolls—a unique collection during that period of history.

## Theocritus

The Museum also supported original writers producing new works. One of these poets was the Greek Theocritus (born c. 300 BCE), who became famous in the third century BCE for his sophisticated verses that extolled the pleasures of an idealized pastoral life. The Arcadian landscape depicted by Theocritus was filled with amorous shepherds and shepherdesses who frolicked to the sound of melodious music. This view of the countryside was in complete contrast to the archaic tradition of Arcadia, in which the countryside was rugged and inhabited by fearsome mythological beasts. This new view of Arcadia found favor with the citizens of Alexandria who, oppressed by the stench, noise, and crowds of city life, began to idealize life in the countryside. It is a view of Arcadia that was to be handed down from Theocritus to the Roman poet Virgil, and from him to the

*This vase illustration shows the Greek hero Odysseus with the blind soothsayer Tiresias. The existing version of Homer's Odyssey was written down by scholars working in Alexandria.*

poets of the Renaissance period, including William Shakespeare.

Theocritus also wrote comedies, one of the very few genres in which the Hellenistic writers were noted for their originality. The ancient comedy of Attica had been a kind of satirical revue, often politically based, and covered contemporary issues. The comedies of the Alexandrian poets, on the other hand, had tightly structured plots that owed nothing to the current political scene. Instead, they told stories of real life, albeit with highly stereotypical characters.

One famous contemporary of these Alexandrian comic writers was the playwright Menander (c. 341–291 BCE). He was very popular in Egypt, and several of his plays have been discovered there on papyrus scrolls. Many attempts were made to persuade him to join the Museum in Alexandria, but Menander preferred to stay in his native Athens.

## The pure sciences

Study of the sciences also came into their own at Ptolemy's academy. The Library of Alexandria was filled with the output of the Museum's scientists as well as its writers. One of the foremost mathematicians in Alexandria around 300 BCE was Euclid, who produced a major work— the *Elements*, which was a compilation of all mathematical knowledge that existed at the time. The work was assembled in 13 books and had a particular emphasis on geometry. This synthesis of everything that had gone before was a typical product of Hellenistic science. Euclid's book was an essential basis for all later mathematical studies. The sections on plane geometry were turned into a school textbook that was used as late as the end of the 19th century CE.

The discoveries of the Greek mathematicians were not always original— many had already been made by the Egyptians or Babylonians. What the

*The playwright Menander was popular in Egypt in the late fourth and early third centuries BCE.*

Greeks did realize, however, was that theorems could be linked, and that geometry was an integrated system that could be studied through the use of logic.

Mathematics was put to little practical use. Only those with something to construct, such as temple architects, knew how to use mathematics to help them in their work. One reason that applied mathematics was ignored was that technology was still in its infancy, and there was little incentive to develop it. Since the sheer brute strength of animals and slaves was enough to construct buildings and turn mill wheels, society could keep going without it. Another factor that worked against the development of technology was the dismissive attitude usually displayed by the Greek elite toward practical matters. It was felt that anything to do with manual labor—and that included technology—was not worthy of the attention of the learned.

One invention in particular could have had a huge effect on the course of history if its implications had been recognized. The scientist Hero of Alexandria discovered the principle of the steam turbine in the first century CE and used it to construct an amusing little steam toy to entertain his friends. The principle was never put to further use, however.

## Archimedes

One ancient Greek citizen who did not ignore the opportunities offered by putting the sciences to practical use was the mathematician and inventor Archimedes (c. 287–212 BCE). Archimedes studied at the Museum in Alexandria before returning to his native Syracuse. He made a particular study of the characteristics of force. It was already known that heavy loads were easier to lift with the help of pulleys and levers, but Archimedes discovered that even the heaviest weight could be lifted easily by using a long lever that moved around a fixed point, or fulcrum.

Archimedes applied this knowledge to many applications, including military catapults. He is also said to have single-handedly launched a massive ship with the help of levers and pulleys. Legend has it that he once boasted: "Give me a solid place to stand in space, and I will move the Earth."

*This relief sculpture depicts the mathematician Euclid. His book, the Elements, was one of the most important works produced in Alexandria.*

### Eureka!

Another famous myth tells the story of one of Archimedes' most famous discoveries, that of specific gravity. The king of Syracuse had asked him to find out whether a supposedly golden crown was in fact pure gold. As water slopped out of the overfull bath when Archimedes got in, it came to him that the amount of water displaced by objects of different volumes would also be different. For this reason, the amount of water displaced by the crown (if it was adulterated) would be different from the amount of water displaced by a lump of pure gold that weighed the same as the crown. Archimedes is reputed to have jumped out of the bath and run down the street naked crying "Eureka!" ("I have found it!").

## Astronomy

Rather than thinking that the stars were controlled by the gods, as earlier civilizations had believed, the Greeks adopted a scientific approach to astronomical study. They employed mathematics, particularly geometry, to help explain the movements of the heavenly bodies. The Greeks were pioneers in making careful observations of the heavens, and they noted that the stars remained in approximately the same place in relation to each other throughout the year, while the moon and five other bodies (Mercury, Venus, Mars, Jupiter, and Saturn) seemed to move around the sky. The Greeks called these heavenly bodies *planates*, after the Greek word meaning "wanderer."

In order to explain the movement of the planets, Greek astronomers put forward the theory that the cosmos was divided into concentric spheres, each one the path of a planet. They usually assumed Earth to be at the center of these spheres (a geocentric view of the universe), which was an error that made the calculations very complicated. One astronomer, Aristarchus of Samos (flourished c. 275 BCE), suggested that everything would be easier to explain if it was assumed that the sun was the central point of the universe, but his ideas were too revolutionary for their time; they were dismissed in favor of the more popular geocentric model.

The geocentric view of the universe was refined in the second century CE by Claudius Ptolemaeus (also known as Ptolemy of Alexandria), who lived from 90 to 168 CE. He used geometric calculations to show that the sun, the moon, and the planets moved in small circular orbits (which he called epicycles) around larger circles, like rings strung on a bracelet. To support his contention that Earth was at the center of these circles, he provided mathematical calculations that were accepted by other astronomers up to the 16th century CE. The calculations were then rejected by Polish

*In this 19th-century-CE woodcut, Hero of Alexandria shows his steam engine, the aeolipile, to his friends. Hero lived in the first century CE. The first truly practical steam engine was not invented until 1,600 years later.*

great work *Geography*, he drew maps of the known world that incorporated lines of latitude and longitude. In spite of being based on incomplete data, these maps were used for centuries. He built a device to study light and presented a mathematical theory of its properties in his treatise *Optics*. In *Harmonica*, he offered an outline of music theory, while in *Tetrabiblos*, he used his knowledge of astronomy and astrology to make predictions about the future.

Another Greek mathematician who contributed a great deal to the knowledge of astronomy was Eratosthenes of Cyrene, who was director of the Library of Alexandria from around 240 to 196 BCE. After distinguishing himself by cataloging 675 stars, Eratosthenes set about trying to calculate the circumference of Earth. He discovered that at the summer solstice a stick placed vertically in the ground in Syene (now Aswan) in Egypt would cast no shadow at noon, while a similar stick in Alexandria would cast a shadow one-fifth of its length. Using this data, Eratosthenes calculated the Earth's circumference, with only 3.5 percent error.

## Medical science

Great advances were made in medical science in Alexandria in the fourth century BCE. They were based on the rational approach to medicine pioneered by Hippocrates of Kos (c. 460–377 BCE), who is called the father of medicine. Previously, the practice of medicine had been bound up with religion and magic. However, Hippocrates believed that disease had natural causes. He considered medicine to be an art that people could learn, diagnosing disease through an examination of the patient.

Hippocrates was born on the Greek island of Kos, where he eventually established a school of medicine. His method of clinical observation was to influence

**The mathematician Archimedes is famous for discovering the concept of specific gravity while in the bath. This drawing is based on a 16th-century-CE engraving.**

astronomer Nicolaus Copernicus, who postulated a heliocentric (sun-centered) view of the cosmos that retained Ptolemy's system of epicycles.

Ptolemy also contributed to several other fields of knowledge. He added to the understanding of trigonometry, using this knowledge to make astrolabes (instruments used for measuring the altitude of the stars) and sundials. In his all succeeding generations of doctors, while his *Regimen in Acute Diseases* introduced the concept of preventive medicine through healthy diet and lifestyle. Hippocrates also suggested that the weather and drinking water can have an effect on public health.

The 70 works generally known as the Hippocratic Collection may not have been written by Hippocrates himself, but they originated from his school of medicine. Similarly, he probably was not the author of the Hippocratic Oath—the oath to act ethically that is taken by all doctors today on graduation.

Herophilus, the personal physician to Ptolemy I in the fourth century BCE, is considered the father of the study of human anatomy. Born in Chalcedon in Anatolia around 335 BCE, he spent most of his life in Alexandria. By dissecting dead bodies, he discovered that the brain is the center of the nervous system. He also identified the separate functions of the motor and sensory nerves. He studied the liver, genitalia, eyes, pancreas, and salivary glands and pioneered research on the blood vessels, learning that they carried blood and not air, as even Hippocrates had believed. Erasistratus (born c. 275 BCE) also carried out many dissections at his school of anatomy in Alexandria and identified the pumping function of the heart, even though he did not understand the concept of the circulation of the blood.

## Philosophy

In addition to advances in literature, the sciences, and medicine, the fourth and third centuries BCE saw the development of several new philosophical movements, including Skepticism, Stoicism, and Epicureanism.

By the fourth century BCE, a number of Greek philosophical schools of thought had been established, including that of Sophism. Traveling teachers of philosophy, politics, and rhetoric, the Sophists thought it was more important to be able to argue on either side of a question than to be morally right.

**The Dance of Apollo with the Muses,** *by Baldassare Peruzzi, was painted in the early 16th century CE. The Temple of the Muses in Alexandria was one of the most important centers of the arts and sciences in the ancient world.*

411

Plato (428–348 BCE) and his student Aristotle (384–322 BCE) objected to the Sophists' view that truth and morality were matters of opinion and countered that view with the concept of idealism. Plato maintained that the object of knowledge (the "idea") was fixed, permanent, and unchangeable. He considered that only this "idea" was real and rejected the view that knowledge was based on the experience of the senses.

The Skeptics countered by saying that all knowledge is questionable and that inquiry itself is a process of doubting. A philosophical school based on these ideas was founded by Pyrrhon of Elis (c. 363–272 BCE). The essence of its philosophy was the impossibility of obtaining certain knowledge. Pyrrhon assumed that mankind primarily strives for happiness, and this is the sole reason for the practice of philosophy. He said that no human could ever know the real nature of things; therefore, the wise person would suspend judgment. Pyrrhon never took sides, believing solely in the value of observation—*skepsis* in Greek. His followers were called Skeptics, and their questioning of everything, based on the example of the questions and answers of Socrates, gave rise to the modern connotation of the word *skeptic*.

## Epicureanism

Epicureanism was founded by the Greek philosopher Epicurus (341–270 BCE), who was born on the island of Samos. When he was 18, he had to go to Athens to do his military service. When his service was completed, he traveled for 10 years, studying and developing his own philosophical ideas. Around 311 BCE, he established a school of philosophy at Mytilene on the island of Lesbos. Later, in 306 BCE, he settled in Athens, where he bought a house with a garden. He set up a school in the garden, and many of his followers from his travels in Anatolia flocked there.

Epicurus's philosophy was based on a system of ethics and the belief that good and evil were to be perceived through the senses. To achieve a happy life, one should seek pleasure and avoid pain. However, he also taught that a simple life was best, because any attempt to satisfy all desires would itself bring pain. So, although the goal of life was pleasure (and intellectual pleasure was to be preferred to sensual pleasure), moderation was the path to true happiness. He described justice, honesty, and friendship as virtues, while politics was to be avoided because it produced only misery.

Epicurus subscribed to the atomic theory refined by Democritus in the fifth century BCE. According to this theory, everything is composed of tiny unchangeable atoms, which join together to form material objects. Epicurus maintained that the soul and the body

## THE MUSES

In Greek mythology, the Muses were nine goddesses thought to inspire artists of all kinds, including philosophers, poets, and musicians. The Muses were all born of a union between Zeus, king of the gods, and Mnemosyne, the goddess of memory. Each Muse presided over a different art or science. Poetry was so important that it had four separate Muses: Polyhymnia for sacred poetry, Calliope for epic poetry, Erato for love poetry, and Euterpe for lyric poetry. Terpsichore was the Muse in charge of choral singing and dance, while Thalia was the Muse for comedy, and Melpomene was the Muse of tragedy. Clio presided over history, and Urania presided over astronomy.

The companions to the Muses were Apollo, the god of music, and the Graces, who were the three goddesses of beauty, joy, and charm. The Graces were also daughters of Zeus, but by the nymph Eurynome. Thalia was associated with good cheer, Aglaia with splendor, and Euphrosyne with mirth.

are composed of material atoms, and when the body dies, the soul is also dissipated and no longer exists. Consequently, there can be no afterlife, and there is nothing to fear from death.

Epicurus did not deny the existence of the gods, but he considered them irrelevant to human affairs. He viewed them as existing in empty space outside the cosmos and believed that they were too caught up in their own affairs to be interested in the material world of mortals. To fear or venerate them was as pointless as fearing life after death.

Followers of Epicurus lived a comparatively austere life in his school. They consumed little other than bread and water and enjoyed few pleasures beyond those of friendship and intellectual pursuits. This modest lifestyle, withdrawn from the world, is in direct contrast to the modern understanding of the word *epicurean*, which has come to mean the pursuit of pleasure; an epicure is someone who indulges freely in the pleasures of food and wine.

## Stoicism

Around 308 BCE, the philosopher Zeno of Cyprus began giving public lectures in Athens under the painted colonnade next to the agora. The colonnade was known as the Stoa Poikile in Greek, which gave the name Stoicism to his teachings. Zeno had studied with the Cynics, at Plato's Academy, and at Aristotle's Lyceum, but he developed his own view of life and the universe.

The Stoics believed that everything in the universe, including mankind, was

*This bust depicts the Greek philosopher Epicurus, who gave his name to a school of philosophy— Epicureanism.*

linked by a divine force (Logos), which they also called reason. Zeno considered that by living in conformity with nature, mankind would live in conformity with the Logos, and this was the only way to attain happiness. By calmly accepting everything that life deals out, mankind can be freed from passion, grief, and joy.

Zeno believed that information received through the senses is based on correct perceptions. If mistakes are made, they are due to inaccurate observation or faulty processing of the information. The person who uses his reason to digest information will come to a correct conception of things. Once one has a correct conception of virtue, one can then gain virtue.

## Equality for all

The Stoics believed that because all mankind is animated by the Logos, all men and women, rich or poor, free or slave, should be treated as equals. This was a revolutionary idea in the third century BCE.

The Stoics considered possessions and wealth unimportant in human relationships and believed that people had a responsibility to help one another. For this reason, they encouraged people to enter public life because it allowed them to improve the lot of their fellow citizens. Stoicism, as first taught by Zeno and later refined by his follower Cleanthes and his successor Chrysippus, was destined to become a major influence in the Roman world.

---

**See also:**

After Alexander (volume 3, page 396) • The Great Philosophers (volume 3, page 352)

# TIME LINE

| GREEK WORLD | | REST OF THE WORLD | |
|---|---|---|---|
| **c. 2000 BCE** | Indo-European peoples arrive in Greece, bringing worship of a sky god who later becomes known as Zeus. | **c. 2000 BCE** | Bronze Age begins in northern Africa. Rice cultivated by Phung Nguyen culture in northern Vietnam. Long-shan culture evolves in Yellow River Valley in China. |
| **c. 1250 BCE** | Dorians begin migrations to mainland Greece. Their main god, Apollo, later becomes major deity in Greek pantheon. | **c. 900 BCE** | Etruscan civilization develops in central Italy. |
| **c. 800 BCE** | Poet Homer believed to have written *Iliad* and *Odyssey* around this time. | | |
| **c. 750 BCE** | Delphi becomes home to cult dedicated to god Apollo; oracle later established at site. | **753 BCE** | Traditional date given for founding of Rome by Romulus; event almost certainly mythical. |
| **c. 657 BCE** | Cypselus drives out rulers of Corinth to establish tyranny in city. | | |
| **625 BCE** | Periander takes over rule of Corinth from father, Cypselus. | **c. 625 BCE** | Large settlement forms between Palatine Hill and Capitoline Hill; gradually develops into city of Rome. |
| **c. 600 BCE** | Mystery cult revolving around story of Persephone established at town of Eleusis. Athenian statesman Solon makes changes to Athenian society, including abolishing debt slavery. | **c. 600 BCE** | Iron Age arrives in northern Europe. City of Teotihuacán emerges in Mexico. |

**c. 800 BCE**

| GREEK WORLD | REST OF THE WORLD |
|---|---|
| | **c. 586 BCE** Jerusalem captured by Babylonians. |
| **582 BCE** Periander's nephew Psammetichus deposed following rebellion; Corinth now ruled by oligarchy. | |
| **c. 575 BCE** Thales establishes school of philosophy in Miletus. He is first of three great philosophers of School of Miletus, other two being Anaximander and Anaximenes. | |
| | **c. 563 BCE** Siddharta Gautama (later known as the Buddha) born. |
| **561 BCE** Peisistratus imposes himself as dictator of Athens for first time; twice driven from city. | **551 BCE** Kongqiu (known in West as Confucius) born. |
| **c. 550 BCE** Thespis, first known playwright, active around this time. | |
| **546 BCE** Peisistratus returns to Athens at head of army; establishes tyranny that lasts for 19 years. | |
| **c. 535 BCE** Dionysian festival held for first time in Athens; part of festivities is competition between playwrights. | |
| **c. 530 BCE** Pythagoras sets up school in Croton. He establishes several mathematical principles, including famous theorem about relationship between three sides of a right triangle. | **529 BCE** Cambyses II defeats Egyptian pharaoh at Pelusium; Egypt comes under Persian rule. |

**c. 550 BCE**

| GREEK WORLD | | REST OF THE WORLD | |
|---|---|---|---|
| **510 BCE** | Hippias deposed as tyrant of Athens; Cleisthenes later creates new democratic system of government. | **c. 510 BCE** | Rome becomes republic after overthrow of last king, Tarquin the Proud. |
| **499 BCE** | Anti-Persian rebellion breaks out in Anatolia. | **c. 500 BCE** | Magadha becomes leading state in India. Dong Son culture emerges in Vietnam. |
| **c. 495 BCE** | Pericles born in Athens. | | |
| **490 BCE** | Darius I, king of Persia, sends army into Greece; Persians defeated at Battle of Marathon. | **c. 490 BCE** | Chinese philosopher Lao-tzu dies. |
| | | **c. 483 BCE** | The Buddha dies. |
| **480 BCE** | Second Persian invasion of Greece. Spartan-led army fails to halt Persian advance at Thermopylae. Greek naval victory at Battle of Salamis turns tide of war. | | |
| **479 BCE** | Decisive victory for Greeks at Battle of Plataea effectively ends Persian Wars. | **479 BCE** | Confucius dies. |
| **477 BCE** | Delian League formed; Athens becomes alliance's leading state. | **c. 475 BCE** | Period of the Warring States begins in China. |
| **468 BCE** | Sophocles takes part in his first Dionysian festival; wins competition. | | |
| **c. 460 BCE** | Historian Thucydides born. | | |
| **458 BCE** | *Oresteia* trilogy by Aeschylus wins competition at Dionysian festival. | **c. 450 BCE** | Iberians learn art of producing iron. |

**c. 500 BCE**

| | GREEK WORLD | | REST OF THE WORLD | |
|---|---|---|---|---|
| | **449 BCE** | Peace treaty finally signed between Greece and Persia. | | |
| | **447 BCE** | Work begins on construction of Parthenon, temple to Athena on Acropolis in Athens. | | |
| | **446 BCE** | Athens and Sparta sign pact known as Thirty Years' Peace. | | |
| | **443 BCE** | Pericles becomes *strategos* for first time. | | |
| | **431 BCE** | Peloponnesian War begins between Athens and Sparta. Euripides' play *Medea* performed for first time. | | |
| **430 BCE** | **430 BCE** | Plague breaks out in Athens. | | |
| | **429 BCE** | Pericles dies. | | |
| | **427 BCE** | *Revellers*, debut comedy by Aristophanes, first produced. | | |
| | **421 BCE** | Peace of Nicias signed by Athens and Sparta; lasts for three years only. | **c. 420 BCE** | Nabateans establish a kingdom in western Arabia, with its capital at Petra in what is now Jordan. |
| | **415 BCE** | Athenians launch naval attack on city of Syracuse in Sicily; campaign ends in failure. | **410 BCE** | Carthaginian colonies in Iberian Peninsula revolt against their rulers. |
| | **404 BCE** | Peloponnesian War ends with defeat of Athens. | | |

| GREEK WORLD | | REST OF THE WORLD | |
| --- | --- | --- | --- |
| **399 BCE** | Socrates charged with heresy; found guilty and sentenced to death. | | |
| **387 BCE** | Plato establishes Academy in Athens. Among his greatest works are *Laws* and *Republic*. | **c. 383 BCE** | Buddhists split into two factions at council in Vaishali. |
| **371 BCE** | Thebes defeats Sparta at Battle of Leuctra. | **c. 371 BCE** | Birth of Confucian philosopher Mencius. |
| **356 BCE** | Alexander the Great born in Pella, Macedonia. | **358 BCE** | Rome becomes head of new Latin League after overcoming alliance of Latin towns in battle. |
| | | **c. 350 BCE** | Cities and states develop among the Maya people of Central America. Crossbow invented in China. |
| | | **c. 343 BCE** | Persian forces under Artaxerxes III reconquer Egypt. |
| **336 BCE** | Alexander defeats army of Greek allies at Chaeronea; ascends to throne of Macedonia following assassination of father, Philip II. | | |
| **c. 335 BCE** | Aristotle, student of Plato, establishes Lyceum in Athens; scientific subjects such as biology and physics taught alongside philosophy. | **c. 335 BCE** | Darius III becomes king of Persia. |
| **334 BCE** | Alexander crosses Dardanelles to begin campaign of conquest in Anatolia; defeats Persian army at Granicus River. | | |

**c. 350 BCE**

| | GREEK WORLD | | REST OF THE WORLD |
|---|---|---|---|
| **332 BCE** | Alexander the Great seizes Tyre and founds city of Alexandria in Egypt. | | |
| **326 BCE** | Macedonian army defeats Indian force at Hydaspes to expand Alexander's empire to Indus Valley. | | |
| **323 BCE** | Alexander dies from fever. | | |
| **322 BCE** | Antipater crushes Aetolian rebels at Battle of Crannon. | **321 BCE** | Mauryan period begins in Magadha, India. |
| **c. 308 BCE** | Zeno of Cyprus begins giving lectures in Athens; teachings form basis of school of philosophy known as Stoicism. | | |
| **306 BCE** | Antigonus and son Demetrius Poliorcetes declare themselves joint kings and successors of Alexander the Great. | | |
| **305 BCE** | Ptolemy proclaims himself king of Egypt. | | |
| **c. 300 BCE** | Ptolemy I expands Temple of the Muses in Alexandria to establish center for arts and sciences. | **c. 300 BCE** | Tiwanaku civilization emerges in Andes. |
| **c. 275 BCE** | Aristarchus of Samos suggests Earth orbits around sun, instead of sun orbiting around Earth. | **264 BCE** | Siege of Messana by King Hiero of Syracuse prompts First Punic War. |
| **c. 250 BCE** | Aristotle studies at Museum in Alexandria, Egypt. | **c. 250 BCE** | Jomon period ends in Japan. Theravada Buddhism established in Ceylon. |

*(Left margin label: **c. 300 BCE**)*

# GLOSSARY

**Achaemenids** Persian 27th dynasty of Egypt (525–404 BCE); founded by Cambyses II of Persia and named after his family, the Achaemenids. Darius I was a member of this dynasty.

**acropolis** fortified part of an ancient Greek city. The most famous such fortress is the Acropolis in Athens, where various large temples were built, including the Parthenon.

**Adonis** in Greek mythology, a young mortal man of outstanding beauty; favorite of Aphrodite.

**Aegean Sea** part of the Mediterranean Sea that separates mainland Greece from Asia Minor (part of modern Turkey).

**Alcmaeonidae** influential Athenian political family during the lifetime of Peisistratus.

**Alexandria** greatest city of the ancient world. It lies on the Mediterranean Sea on the western edge of the delta of the Nile River and was founded in 332 BCE by Alexander the Great.

**Anatolia** another name for Asia Minor (part of modern Turkey).

**Antigonids** descendants of Demetrius Poliorcetes; ruling dynasty of Macedonia from 306 to 168 BCE.

**Apollo** Greek god of the sun, oracles, music, poetry, and justice; son of Zeus. The god of medicine, Apollo could also choose to inflict disease as punishment.

**Aramaic** Semitic language that was widely spoken in western Asia until displaced by Greek after the conquests of Alexander the Great.

**Arcadia** mountainous region of the central Peloponnese, Greece.

*archons* magistrates in Athens, beginning around the seventh century BCE. Elected annually, their duties comprised legislation, the dispensation of justice, the conduct of religion, and military affairs.

**Artemisium, Battle of** Persian naval victory over the Greeks in 480 BCE.

**Athens** preeminent city-state of ancient Greece.

**Attica** region of central Greece. Its chief city was Athens.

**Babylon** city in southern Mesopotamia that was the center of an Amorite empire under Hammurabi. Later, Babylon continued as the cultural and political capital of the region. From 612 to 539 BCE, Babylon was the capital of the Neo-Babylonian Empire.

**Bacchiads** aristocratic family that ruled the city-state of Corinth in the seventh century BCE.

**Bosporus** strait, 19 miles (30 km) long, that joins the Black Sea and the Sea of Marmara.

**Byzantium** ancient Greek city on the shore of the Bosporus; later known as Constantinople; modern Istanbul.

**Chaeronea, Battle of** conflict in which Philip II of Macedon defeated Thebes and Athens in 338 BCE.

**Chalcedon** ancient port on the Bosporus; overshadowed by its proximity to Byzantium.

*choregi* Greek sponsors of theatrical productions and competitions.

**comedy** originally, any play or literary composition with a nontragic ending.

*comos* procession of Greek citizens during which they wore masks and danced and sang; often part of festivals in honor of Dionysus.

**Corcyra** ancient name for the Greek island of Corfu.

**Corinth** city of the Peloponnese, around 50 miles (80 km) west of Athens.

**Corinthian War** conflict that lasted from 395 to 387 BCE between Sparta and an alliance among Thebes, Athens, Corinth, and Argos, initially supported by Persia.

**Corupedium, Battle of** fought in 281 BCE, the decisive final confrontation between the rival successors to Alexander the Great.

**Council of 500** originally conceived by Cleisthenes and fully realized by Solon, a political decision-making body in Athens consisting of 10 groups, each of 50 men, chosen by lot.

**Crannon, Battle of** military confrontation in 322 BCE in which Macedonian forces under Antipater defeated rebellious Greek forces led by the Athenians.

**crop rotation** farming system in which fields are divided into groups (typically of three) in which a different one is left fallow every year so that it may regenerate.

**Croton** Greek colony in southern Italy in which Pythagoras settled around 530 BCE.

**Cynics** from the Greek *kunikoi*. Followers of Diogenes and

Antisthenes, they protested the material interests of established society. Holding virtue to be the only good, they stressed independence from worldly needs and pleasures and led austere lives.

**Cyrenaica** coastal district of southern Mediterranean Sea; former Greek colony; now part of Libya.

**Delian League** military alliance set up in 477 BCE to protect the Greek cities of Ionia (part of modern Turkey) against attack by the Persians.

**Delos** one of the Cyclades, a group of islands in the Aegean Sea.

**Delphi** city in central Greece; site of an Apollo sanctuary and an oracle. The utterances of Pythia, the priestess of the oracle, had great influence on personal and political life.

**democracy** from the Greek *demos* (people) and *kratein* (to rule); government by the people, either directly or through elected representatives. This form of government arose at the end of the sixth century BCE in Athens.

**diadochs** military commanders who succeeded Alexander the Great.

**Dionysia** Greek annual festival in honor of Dionysus; characterized by processions, poetry competitions, and theatrical performances.

**Dionysus** Greek god of wine, ecstasy, reproduction, life force, chaos, and death.

*dithyramb* ancient Greek hymn of praise to the god Dionysus.

**Dodona** site, near Epirus in north-western Greece, of an oracle devoted to the god Zeus.

**Dorians** people from Macedonia and northern Greece who conquered parts of the Peloponnese and Crete between 1200 and 1000 BCE.

*ecclesia* the tribal meeting of Athens open to all citizens that, after Cleisthenes' reforms, made the final political decisions on internal and foreign affairs.

**Elea** ancient town in Italy founded by Greek refugees; famous for its school of philosophy; modern Velia.

**Eleusis** city on the Greek coast near Athens where mysteries were held between around 600 and 400 BCE.

**Ephesus** Ionian city in ancient Anatolia (part of modern Turkey).

**Epicureanism** philosophy founded by Epicurus (341–270 BCE). Its central tenets were the pursuit of happiness and the avoidance of pain.

**Epidamnus** colony on the Adriatic coast in part of what is now Albania; founded in the fifth century BCE by Greeks from Corcyra.

**Epidaurus** small but important city-state of ancient Greece; situated in the northeastern Peloponnese.

**Eurymedon** river in Asia Minor; site of a major battle in 466 BCE between the Persians and the Delian League.

**Gaugamela, Battle of** military confrontation in 331 BCE in which Alexander the Great defeated Darius III of Persia.

**Gordian knot** according to Greek legend, a complex knot that could only be untied by the man destined to become king of Asia. The young Alexander the Great cut it with one blow of his sword.

**Granicus River, Battle of** military confrontation between Alexander the Great and the Persian Empire near Troy in Asia Minor in 334 BCE.

**Hades** god of the underworld and brother of Zeus; also the name of the underworld itself.

**Hanukkah** Jewish midwinter festival that commemorates the restoration of Jewish rites in the temple at Jerusalem by Judas Maccabaeus.

**hemlock** poisonous herb; commonly thought to have been the cause of Socrates's death.

**Heracles** greatest and strongest of Greek mythological heroes; also known as Hercules.

**Hermes** Greek god of travelers, shepherds, trade, and cunning. The son of Zeus and the messenger of the gods, he guided souls to the underworld.

**hoplites** soldiers in the Greek heavy infantry, armed with swords, lances, and the large round shields known as hoplons.

**Illyria** ancient region of the Balkans; part of modern Albania.

**Indo-European languages** common family of European and Asiatic (Indian) languages.

**Ionia** coastal region of southwestern Anatolia (part of modern Turkey) that contained several Greek city-states.

**Ishtar** Semitic war goddess who merged with Inanna and became the goddess of love and fertility.

**isthmus** narrow strip of land, bordered on two sides by water, that joins two larger land masses.

**Jason** Greek mythological hero who sailed in the *Argo* in search of the Golden Fleece.

**Logos** divine force—also known as reason—that the Stoics believed directed the universe and humankind.

**Lydia** ancient province of Anatolia (part of modern Turkey). Its capital was Sardis.

**Macedon** alternatively, Macedonia; region of northeastern Greece that was for a short time during the fourth century BCE the most powerful state in the eastern Mediterranean region.

**Maia** in Greek mythology, the eldest of the Pleiades and the mother of Zeus's son, Hermes.

**Mantinea** ancient city in Arcadia; site of two battles. The first Battle of Mantinea, in 418 BCE, was the largest land battle of the Peloponnesian War. In the second Battle of Mantinea (362 BCE), Thebes defeated the allied forces of Athens and Sparta.

**Marathon** city on the east coast of Attica where the Persians suffered a devastating defeat in 490 BCE by a small Athenian army under Miltiades.

**Medes** Indo-European people who entered northeastern Iran around the 17th century BCE.

**Mesopotamia** area in western Asia surrounding the Euphrates and Tigris rivers. Floods and irrigation made the the land fertile, and around 4500 BCE, the first agricultural settlements were founded there.

**Minoan civilization** Bronze Age civilization on Crete.

**Muses** in Greek—and later in Roman—mythology, nine sister goddesses (daughters of Zeus) who inspired human artistic creativity: Calliope (epic poetry), Clio (history), Erato (lyric poetry), Euterpe (music), Melpomene (tragedy), Polyhymnia (sacred poetry), Terpsichore (dancing), Thalia (comedy), Urania (astronomy).

**Parnassus** mountain of central Greece; in Greek mythology, the home of Apollo and the Muses.

**Parthenon** temple on the Athenian Acropolis dedicated to Pallas Athena; built between 447 and 438 BCE.

**Peloponnese** large, mountainous peninsula joined to the mainland of Greece by the Isthmus of Corinth.

**Peloponnesian War (431–404 BCE)** conflict of hegemony between Athens (generally allied with the Ionians) and Sparta (allied with the Dorians). The direct cause was a conflict about the island of Corcyra (modern Corfu). The army of Sparta annually destroyed Attica, while the Athenian fleet plundered the Peloponnesian coasts. Sparta finally triumphed over Athens with help from the Persians.

**Pergamum** ancient Greek city in Asia Minor; close to the modern city of Izmir, Turkey.

**Persephone** daughter of Demeter, the goddess of agriculture. Her recurring abduction by Hades and return from the underworld symbolize the growth and decay of life.

**phalanx** a battle formation in the Greek infantry, usually consisting of eight rows of hoplites fighting in extremely close ranks.

**potsherd** fragment of pottery, usually one that has been unearthed by archaeological excavation.

*prytanes* 10 groups of 50 men from the Council of 500; formed the daily administration of Athens for one-month periods.

**rhetors** orator-politicians in Athens. With their rhetorical gifts, they had great influence on Athenian politics.

**Salamis** island on the western coast of Attica where the Persian fleet was defeated by the Greeks in 480 BCE.

**satrap** provincial governor in the Achaemenian Persian Empire.

**satyr play** Greek dramatic work with a heroic mythological theme, like a tragedy, but with a humorous tone and a chorus of satyrs (goatlike male companions of Pan and Dionysus who roamed the woods and mountains). Satyr plays formed the last part of a tetralogy and were thus always performed after three tragedies.

**Seleucid Empire** empire that, between 312 and 64 BCE, extended from Thrace on the edge of the Black Sea to the western border of India. It was formed by Seleucus I Nicator from the remnants of Alexander the Great's realm.

**Skepticism** philosophy based on the assumption that all assumptions should be doubted.

**Sophists** Greek teachers in the fifth century BCE who gave popularized (and eventually denounced) instruction in philosophy, political science, rhetoric, and literature.

**Stoicism** school of philosophy founded by Zeno of Citium in Athens in the third century BCE. At its core is the belief that people should do what is required of them by nature and accept their lot.

**Thermopylae** mountain pass between Thessaly and central Greece where Leonidas and hundreds of Spartans died covering the retreat of the Greek army from the Persians in 480 BCE.

**trireme** ancient galley ship with three banks of oars.

*zeugitai* social class of economically independent farmers in Athens; owners of *zeugos* (yokes of oxen). The *zeugitai* served as foot soldiers in the army and, after Solon's reforms, could hold minor political offices.

# MAJOR HISTORICAL FIGURES

**Aeschylus (525–456 BCE)** Greek playwright; author of the *Oresteia* trilogy and *The Persians*.

**Alcibiades (c. 450–404 BCE)** Athenian politician and military commander whose policies contributed to his city's defeat by Sparta in the Peloponnesian War (431–404 BCE).

**Alexander the Great (356–323 BCE)** king of Macedonia from 336 BCE until his death. Alexander overthrew the Persian Empire and laid the foundations of a Hellenistic Empire.

**Antigonus (382–301 BCE)** Macedonian general who co-founded the Antigonid dynasty.

**Archimedes (c. 287–212 BCE)** Greek mathematician and inventor.

**Aristophanes (c. 450–388 BCE)** early Greek comic playwright.

**Aristotle (384–322 BCE)** Greek philosopher and scientist.

**Croesus** king of Lydia between 560 and 546 BCE; conquered Ionia and was in turn subjugated by the Persians; famous for his vast wealth.

**Cyrus the Great** sixth-century-BCE Persian ruler who founded an empire that stretched from the Aegean Sea eastward to the Indus River.

**Darius I** king of Persia between 521 and 486 BCE; started the First Persian War. His expedition against Athens ended in the Battle of Marathon.

**Democritus** fifth-century-BCE Greek philosopher.

**Diogenes (c. 400–325 BCE)** Greek philosopher; founded Cynicism.

**Eratosthenes** Greek mathematician and astronomer of the third and second centuries BCE who calculated the circumference of Earth.

**Euclid (c. 300 BCE)** ancient Greek mathematician; known as the father of geometry.

**Euripides (c. 485–406 BCE)** Greek dramatist; author of more than 90 plays, including *Medea*.

**Herodotus (born c. 480 BCE)** known as the father of Greek historiography.

**Herophilus** personal physician to Ptolemy I in the fourth century BCE; widely regarded as the father of the study of human anatomy.

**Hesiod (c. 700 BCE)** epic poet; author of *Thegonia*, on religion and mythology, and *Works and Days*, a manual for farmers.

**Hippocrates (c. 460–377 BCE)** ancient Greek physician; known as the father of medicine.

**Homer (c. 800 BCE)** legendary Greek poet to whom the epics the *Iliad* and the *Odyssey* are attributed.

**Judas Maccabaeus** leader of the Maccabaean revolt against the Seleucid Empire (166–165 BCE).

**Leonidas (died 480 BCE)** Spartan king who died in the Battle of Thermopylae.

**Menander (c. 341–291 BCE)** Athenian comic dramatist; author of more than 100 plays.

**Miltiades** general who led Athenian forces to victory over the Persians at the Battle of Marathon in 490 BCE.

**Pericles (c. 495–429 BCE)** democratic leader of Athens during its Golden Age.

**Plato (c. 428–348 BCE)** ancient Greek philosopher who, with Aristotle and Socrates, laid the foundations of subsequent Western thought.

**Plutarch (c. 46–120 CE)** Greek biographer and historian.

**Pythagoras (c. 580–500 BCE)** ancient Greek philosopher and mathematician whose religious, political, and philosophical doctrines strongly influenced Plato.

**Socrates (469–399 BCE)** Athenian philosopher. His ideas were passed down primarily through the writings of Plato.

**Sophocles (c. 496–406 BCE)** Greek playwright; author of tragedies.

**Thucydides (c. 460–400 BCE)** Greek historian of the Peloponnesian War.

**Virgil (70–19 BCE)** Roman poet; author of the *Aeneid*, an epic of the foundation of Rome by fugitives from the sacking of Troy.

**Xenophon (431–350 BCE)** Greek historian; author of the *Anabasis*, an account of how Greek mercenaries attempted to seize the Persian throne.

**Xerxes I** king of Persia between 486 and 465 BCE; destroyed Athens in 480 BCE during the Second Persian War.

**Zeno (c. 335–263 BCE)** Greek Cypriot who founded the Stoic school of philosophy.

# RESOURCES FOR FURTHER STUDY

## BOOKS

Aeschylus (translated by Robert Fagles). *The Oresteia: Agamemnon; The Libation Bearers; The Eumenides.* New York, 1984.

Alcock, Susan E., John F. Cherry, and Jaś Elsner (eds.). *Pausanias: Travel and Memory in Roman Greece.* New York, 2001.

Alexander, Edward P., and Mary Alexander. *Museums in Motion.* Lanham, MD, 2008.

Allen, Reginald E. (ed.). *Greek Philosophy: Thales to Aristotle.* New York, 1991.

Aristophanes (translated by Paul Roche). *The Complete Plays.* New York, 2005.

Aristotle (edited by Richard McKeon). *The Basic Works of Aristotle.* New York, 2001.

Aristotle (translated by Benjamin Jowett). *Politics.* Mineola, NY, 2000.

Bendick, Jeanne. *Archimedes and the Door of Science.* New York, 1962.

Bentwich, Norman De Mattos. *Hellenism.* Philadelphia, PA, 1919.

Biers, William R. *The Archaeology of Greece: An Introduction.* Ithaca, NY, 1996.

Boardman, John. *The Greeks Overseas: Their Early Colonies and Trade.* London, England, 1980.

Boardman, John (ed.). *The Oxford History of Classical Art.* New York, 1993.

Bowersock, Glen W. *Hellenism in Late Antiquity.* Ann Arbor, MI, 1996.

Bury, J.B., and Russell Meiggs. *A History of Greece.* London, England, 1975.

Cartledge, Paul. *Alexander the Great: The Hunt for a New Past.* Woodstock, NY, 2004.

————. *Democritus.* New York, 1999.

Cooper, John M. *Reason and Human Good in Aristotle.* Cambridge, MA, 1975.

Dinsmoor, W.B. *The Architecture of Ancient Greece: An Account of Its Historic Development.* New York, 1975.

Ellis, Walter M. *Alcibiades.* New York, 1989.

Epicurus (translated by Eugene O'Connor). *The Essential Epicurus: Letters, Principal Doctrines, Vatican Sayings, and Fragments.* Buffalo, NY, 1993.

Euripides (translated by Moses Hadas and John McLean). *Ten Plays by Euripides.* New York, 1984.

Fildes, Alan. *Alexander the Great: Son of the Gods.* Los Angeles, CA, 2002.

Forrest, W.G. *The Emergence of Greek Democracy.* London, England, 1966.

Fuller, J.F.C. *The Generalship of Alexander the Great.* New York, 1960.

Geldard, Richard G. *Parmenides and the Way of Truth.* Rhinebeck, NY, 2007.

Gergel, Tania (ed.). *Alexander the Great: Selected Texts from Arrian, Curtius, and Plutarch.* New York, 2004.

Green, Robert. *Alexander the Great.* New York, 1996.

Grube, G.M.A. *Plato's Thought.* Indianapolis, IN, 1980.

Habicht, Christian. *Pausanias' Guide to Ancient Greece.* Berkeley, CA, 1998.

Hadas, Moses. *Greek Drama.* New York, 1965.

Heath, Thomas Little. *Aristarchus of Samos, the Ancient Copernicus: A History of Greek Astronomy to Aristarchus, together with Aristarchus's Treatise on the Sizes and Distances of the Sun and Moon.* Oxford, England, 1913.

Heckel, Waldemar. *The Wars of Alexander the Great, 336–323 BC.* New York, 2003.

Heraclitus (translated by Brooks Haxton). *The Collected Wisdom of Heraclitus.* New York, 2001.

Herodotus (translated by Walter Blanco). *The Histories.* New York, 1992.

Holbl, Gunther. *History of the Ptolemaic Empire.* New York, 2001.

Kagan, Donald. *The Peloponnesian War: Athens and Sparta in Savage Conflict, 431–404 BC.* London, England, 2003.

———. *Pericles of Athens and the Birth of Democracy.* New York, 1991.

Kahn, Charles H. *Anaximander and the Origins of Greek Cosmology.* Indianapolis, IN, 1994.

———. *Pythagoras and the Pythagoreans: A Brief History.* Indianapolis, IN, 2001.

Lasky, Kathryn. *The Librarian who Measured the Earth.* Boston, MA, 1994.

Mogens, Herman Hansen (translated by J.A. Crook). *The Athenian Democracy in the Age of Demosthenes: Structure, Principles, and Ideology.* Norman, OK, 1999.

Morris, Ian. *Burial and Ancient Society: The Rise of the Greek City-State.* New York, 1987.

Morris, Ian (ed.). *Classical Greece: Ancient Histories and Modern Archaeologies.* New York, 1994.

Morrison, J.S., and J.F. Coates. *The Athenian Trireme.* New York, 1986.

O'Grady, Patricia F. *Thales of Miletus: The Beginnings of Western Science and Philosophy.* Burlington, VT, 2002.

Payne, Mark. *Theocritus and the Invention of Fiction.* New York, 2007.

Pindar (translated by Anthony Verity). *The Complete Odes.* New York, 2007.

Plato (translated by Hugh Tredennick and Harold Tarrant). *The Last Days of Socrates.* New York, 1993.

Plato (translated by Allan Bloom). *The Republic of Plato.* New York, 1991.

Pollard, Justin, and Howard Reid. *The Rise and Fall of Alexandria: Birthplace of the Modern Mind.* New York, 2006.

Samons, Loren J., II (ed.). *The Cambridge Companion to the Age of Pericles.* New York, 2007.

Sellars, John. *Stoicism.* London, England, 2006.

Shanks, Michael. *Art and the Early Greek State: An Interpretive Archaeology.* New York, 1999.

Smith, Helaine L. *Masterpieces of Classic Greek Drama.* Westport, CT, 2006.

Sophocles (translated by Richard Claverhouse Jebb). *The Complete Plays of Sophocles.* New York, 1967.

Stone, I.F. *The Trial of Socrates.* New York, 1989.

Strauss, Barry S. *The Battle of Salamis: The Naval Encounter that Saved Greece—and Western Civilization.* New York, 2004.

Temkin, Owsei. *Hippocrates in a World of Pagans and Christians.* Baltimore, MD, 1991.

Theocritus (translated by Anthony Verity). *Idylls.* New York, 2002.

Thucydides (translated by Steven Lattimore). *History of the Peloponnesian War.* Indianapolis, IN, 1998.

Trumble, Kelly. *The Library of Alexandria.* New York, 2003.

Warner, Rex. *Athens at War.* New York, 1971.

Wiles, David. *The Masks of Menander: Sign and Meaning in Greek and Roman Performance.* New York, 1991.

Wycherley, R.E. *The Stones of Athens.* Princeton, NJ, 1978.

Xenophon (translated by Robin Waterfield). *The Expedition of Cyrus.* New York, 2005.

Zannos, Susan. *The Life and Times of Archimedes.* Hockessin, DE, 2005.

# WEB SITES

**Aeschylus**
Biography of the Greek playwright; includes links to all of his works currently in print
*http://www.imagi-nation.com/moonstruck/clsc3.htm*

**Alexander the Great**
Web site that is dedicated to the Macedonian general; includes more than 400 photographs, as well as links to hundreds of additional sites
*http://www.isidore-of-seville.com/Alexanderama.html*

# RESOURCES FOR FURTHER STUDY

**Athenian Democracy**
Analysis of the Athenian political system
*http://www.bbc.co.uk/history/ancient/greeks/greekcritics_01.shtml*

**Delian League**
Web site that details the history of the Athenian confederation
*http://www.bbc.co.uk/dna/h2g2/A14481777*

**Diadochs**
Web site that is dedicated to the lives of the successors to Alexander the Great
*http://www.livius.org/di-dn/diadochi/war02.html*

**Euripides (Biography)**
Short biography of the playwright and numerous links to discussions of his work
*http://www.theatredatabase.com/ancient/euripides_001.html*

**Euripides (Works)**
Includes links to several biographies of the playwright, as well as essays on specific pieces of work
*http://www.gpc.edu/~shale/humanities/literature/world_literature/euripides.html*

**Greek Philosophy**
Contains discussions of all the main schools of Greek philosophical thought
*http://www.iep.utm.edu/g/greekphi.htm*

**Greek Religion**
Resources for the study and understanding of all aspects of ancient Greek religion
*http://www.greekreligion.org*

**Greek Theater**
Features a time line of Greek drama, as well as the texts of a number of key works
*http://academic.reed.edu/humanities/110tech/Theater.html*

**Hellenistic Greece**
Guide to the Hellenistic age
*http://www.wsu.edu/~dee/GREECE/HELLGREE.HTM*

**Judas Maccabeus**
Biography of the Jewish rebel leader
*http://www.jewishencyclopedia.com/view.jsp?artid=672&letter=J*

**Menander**
Introduction to the work of the playwright known as the father of comedy
*http://www.theatrehistory.com/ancient/menander001.html*

**Muses**
Introduction to the functions of the nine Greek goddesses; includes links to material of related interest
*http://ancienthistory.about.com/library/bl/bl_myth_europe_grecoroman_muses.htm*

**Sophocles**
Biography of the ancient Greek playwright
*http://www.imagi-nation.com/moonstruck/clsc1.htm*

**Thermopylae**
Detailed account of one of the key battles in ancient Greek history
*http://www.historynet.com/magazines/military_history/3038411.html*

**Trireme**
History of the development of the Greek warship; includes details of construction techniques
*http://home-3.tiscali.nl/~meester7/engtrireme.html*

# INDEX